BOOK OF REMEMBRANCE

**THIS BOOK IS DEDICATED TO THE MEMORY
OF ALL WHO SERVED IN:**

WORLD WAR I

WORLD WAR II

KOREAN WAR

**FROM PLATTSVILLE, BRIGHT, CHESTERFIELD
AND WASHINGTON**

A gold star identifies those who died for their country

Compiled by Gow Harvey

Printed in Canada

Edited by Gow Harvey and Denise Tew

Cover Design by Peter Marshall

Author Photo by Elliot Ferguson, Sentinel Review, Woodstock

Type design and set-up by Heather Sparks, To The Point Design
Email: sparkswillfly@rogers.com

The publishing of this book was made possible through funds received from:
THE ONTARIO TRILLIUM FOUNDATION

"The Ontario Trillium Foundation, an agency of the Ministry of Culture, receives annually one hundred
million dollars of government funding generated through Ontario's charity casino initiative."

THE ONTARIO TRILLIUM FOUNDATION
LA FONDATION TRILLIUM DE L'ONTARIO

National Library of Canada Cataloguing in Publication

Harvey, Gow, 1923-
        Book of remembrance / Gow Harvey.

Includes index.
ISBN 0-9735307-0-7

        1. Veterans--Ontario--Oxford (County) 2. World War,
1914-1918--Ontario--Oxford (County) 3. World War, 1939-1945--
Ontario--Oxford (County) 4. Korean War, 1950-1953--Ontario--
Oxford (County) 5. Oxford (Ont. : County)--History, Military--
20th century. I. Title.

UA601.O6H37 2004   305.9'0697'0971346   C2004-902357-8

TABLE OF CONTENTS

TABLE OF CONTENTS

FOREWORD

Gow Harvey and Peter Marshall.
Book presentation November 11th 2003.

In casting about for a suitable project to mark the Millennium, students and staff at Plattsville & District Public School decided that their town should have its own cenotaph honoring those from the area who had died while serving in Canada's Armed Forces during World War I and World War II. To that end, the students, from both the Plattsville & District Public School and Plattsville Christian School, raised the funds needed to erect a cenotaph in the park. Some citizens also generously donated.

In keeping with the sentiment behind the cenotaph, and to preserve the memory of those who had served in Canada's wartime military, I thought that a Book of Remembrance recording the names and a brief history of all who served from this area would be helpful. The Book provides such information as I have been able to locate for those men and women who served in World War I (1914-1918), World War II (1939-1945), and the Korean conflict (1950-1953).

It is easy to forget the extraordinary contribution that Canada made during these wars of the Twentieth Century. By 1918, some 600,000 of Canada's 8,000,000 people were in uniform and the Country had lost 60,661 people to combat in the "War to End All Wars". Three decades later, Canada mobilized again, this time putting almost 1,100,00 of its citizens in uniform and producing vast quantities of war material for the Allied armies. Between 1939 and 1945, Canada lost 42,042 of those serving with many others injured or taken prisoner. Of 25,000 Canadian military personnel in Korea, 309 soldiers and 3 sailors lost their lives.

I am indebted to Peter Marshall, the retired Principal of Plattsville & District Public School, for the beautiful wooden cover that he designed and crafted for this Book of Remembrance. I can only hope that copies of this work of art will do justice to the beauty of the original.

The Plattsville & District Heritage Society guided by their President, Wayne Currah, decided to apply to the Trillium Foundation for a grant to fund the printing of this book. Denise Tew was invaluable in filling out the grant application and listing the benefits to the community that this volume would bestow. Without her efforts it is doubtful we would have received funding.

Many other people contributed to this book. From California to Florida, from Cape Breton to Vancouver, and from myriad points between, the friends and relatives of local veterans dug up the records and pictures that I needed to make this book a living testament. I deeply regret that there may be some veterans who I have not been able to trace. Unfortunately some families simply disappear over time.

Two pages have been left blank to record family members or close friends whom you may particularly wish to remember.

Gow Harvey
January 2004

In Flanders Fields

—

In Flanders fields the poppies blow,
Between the crosses, row on row,
That mark our place; and in the sky
The larks, still bravely singing, fly
Scarce heard amid the guns below.

We are the Dead. Short days ago
We lived, felt dawn, saw sunset glow,
Loved, and were loved, and now we lie
            In Flanders fields.

Take up our quarrel with the foe:
To you from failing hands we throw
The torch; be yours to hold it high.
If ye break faith with us who die
We shall not sleep, though poppies grow
            In Flanders fields

Punch
Dec 8 · 1915

John McCrae

—

ii

THE SOLDIER'S
TEN COMMANDMENTS.

1.   When on guard thou shalt challenge all parties approaching thy post, coming to the "on guard" in a determined manner

2.   Thou shalt not send by mail, any likeness of any airships in the heaven above, nor any picture postcard of the earth beneath, nor any drawings of submarines under the sea; for I. the Censor, am a jealous man, visiting the iniquities of the offenders with three months C.B., but showing mercy to thousands who keep my commandments, by suffering their letters to go forth.

3.   Thou shalt not use profane language, unless under extraordinary circumstances, such as seeing thy comrade shot or dropping thy rifle on thy toe when ordering arms, or getting petrol in thy tea.

4.   Remember the Sabbeth Day is part of the soldier's week, six days shalt thou labour and do all thy work, and the seventh day do all thy odd jobs.

5.   Honour thy King and Country; keep your rifle well oiled, and shoot straight, that thy days may be long in the land which the enemy giveth thee.

6.   Thou shalt not steal (thy comrades kit).

7.   Thou shalt not kill (time).

8.   Thou shalt not adulterate thy mess tin by using it for a shaving mug.

9.   Thou shalt not bear false witness against thy comrade; but preserve thy discreet silence on his outgoings and incomings

10.   Thou shalt not covet the Sergeant's post nor the Corporal's, nor the S.M's., but do thy duty, and by dint of perseverence rise to the high position of—Field Marshal.

Further a new commandment I give unto you:—Love thy rifle as thyself, and "Steady Johnny steady: keep your head down low".

Reprint=1916.

My Two Minutes

In my two minutes of silence,
I'm taken back in time.
With boys from across Canada,
That became brothers of mine.
What province you came from,
Made no difference to us.
For there on our shoulder,
Was the word Canada.
We talked of our homes,
And how we grew up.
Of our brothers and sisters,
Mom, Dad and our pups.

We talked, what would we do,
When we got home.
Well some of us made it,
While others still roam.
My medals remind me,
Where all have been.
And the faces of men,
Never more to be seen.
My two minutes of silence,
Has come to its end.
The bugle is sounding,
And it is saying Amen.

Roy JJ Blackmore
RJJB.

A Child

A child stood by a cenotaph,
Not really knowing why.
All the adults were very quiet,
And tears were in their eyes.
The silence then was broken,
By a bugle sounding near.
And sounds of reveille,
Came drifting Oh so clear.
Then a voice was heard so softly,
Let us give thanks to those.

Whom died in the battles,
So many years ago.
The little child bowed it's head,
And remembered a little friend.
Who's Daddy died not long ago,
And they miss him to no end.
They gave the greatest gift of all,
Their live's for you and me.
So hold your child real close,
It's a gift from God and We.

Roy JJ Blackmore
RJJB.

We Remember

We remember the soldiers that died,

They fought and listened to people cry.

From this day we lay our work aside,

We say our poems and watch everyone cry,

So we can remember the soldiers that died.

Written at 14 years old by Casey Blackmore, Grand Daughter of Roy Blackmore.

The Bugle

The bugle's sounding,

To bring us near.

To those we lost,

And knew so dear.

The bugle's sounding,

And we're left here.

They gave a lifetime,

And we just tears.

The bugle's sounding,

And we give them not.

But two minutes,

By the clock.

Roy J J Blackmore
RJJB.

OXFORD RIFLES MILITIA MEMBERS FROM PLATTSVILLE WERE BUSSED TO WOODSTOCK FOR TRAINING TWO NIGHTS A WEEK IN THE EARLY PART OF THE WAR. THERE WAS A PLATOON OF MEN FROM PLATTSVILLE AND THIS PICTURE WAS TAKEN OF THEM WAITING IN FRONT OF THE J.B. ENGLISH GENERAL STORE FOR TRANSPORTATION TO THE WOODSTOCK ARMOURY. (1939-1940)

PLATTSVILLE SERVICEMEN AND WOMEN, WORLD WAR 1, AUGUST 11, 1919
BACK ROW–WALLACE MCDONALD, UNKNOWN, HENRY CHRISTENSEN, ARTHUR WARWICK, BILL BROWN, GEORGE ALDRIDGE, J. CHRISTENSEN MIDDLE ROW–TOM PRATT, ROSS VEITCH, MISS SCOTT, PERRY HALL, –SCOTT FRONT ROW–JACK SANGWIN, LESLIE BRICKER, –HAMACHER, LYLE HARMER, SYDNEY GREEN

GROESBEEK WAR MEMORIAL CEMETERY IN HOLLAND 1,300 CANADIANS KILLED AT THE END OF THE SECOND WORLD WAR ARE BURIED HERE. EACH GRAVE IS BEAUTIFULLY TENDED BY ONE OF THE LOCAL SCHOOL CHILDREN.

GROESBEEK WAR GRAVES

Margaret Fairburn Scott and Agnes Craig Bell

SCOTT Margaret Fairburn and BELL Agnes Craig

Margaret Fairburn Scott was born on May 8th 1871 to John and Elizabeth (nee-Lockie) Scott. Agnes Craig Bell was born on April 30th 1883 to Andrew and Margaret (nee-Little) Bell.

Neither of them were married and in those days the only suitable employment for unmarried ladies was teaching or nursing. They heard of a Miss Blair from Ratho who was training as a nurse in St. Louis, Missouri, so in the early part of the century off to St. Louis they went. The training period was three years. After graduation, they went back to Chesterfield and nursed there in the summer but returned to Missouri in the winter. When the war started nurses were needed in the Canadian Army. Margaret and Agnes enlisted in the beginning of 1917. Their first stop was Kingston where all nurses received the rank of Lieutenant. Each received her medical, was vaccinated for small pox and inoculated for typhoid. In early 1917 Margaret and Agnes landed in France. The hospitals were in converted buildings, huts and tents. Conditions were appalling. Mud was a constant as were the rats and lice. The nurses had to wash their hair in kerosene to kill the lice. Agnes nursed at a hospital near Rouen and at #7 General Hospital near St. Omers. The dedication and skill of these ladies of mercy was incredible. Of the 167,000 wounded only 13,289 died of their wounds, a remarkable recovery rate of 93%. Without proper facilities and nothing in the way of antibiotics, the doctors and nurses performed miracles. Many contracted diseases from the patients and Agnes was stricken a few times. With the last of their patients they were returned to Canada.

One of the most emotional duties nurses undertook was writing to the next of kin of soldiers who had died of their wounds. Agnes received her honourable discharge on January 31st 1920 and Margaret about the same time.

After the war, Agnes Bell went to Toronto and served as a Public School Nurse. There she met David Monroe Ross, the Member of Legislative Assembly (M.L.A.) for Oxford County. They fell in love and were married on January 1st 1927 in the Chesterfield Church. They settled down on the lovely farm called Kirkhill near Embro. A son, Hugh Monroe, was born on August 30th 1928. Agnes died on March 8th 1962.

On a visit to California, Margaret Scott met Thomas Graham, a distant cousin. He was a raconteur of some note. Thomas had been married twice before and had a son by his second wife. After a short courtship he and Margaret were married and moved to Seattle, Washington. Margaret continued nursing in Seattle. Maggie loved to tell stories about witches and could keep children enthralled. One summer in the 1920's she drove all the way from Seattle to Chesterfield in a Model T Ford. The roads in those days were mud or gravel so it was a challenging trip. Sadly Maggie developed cancer and died in 1932. She was brought home for burial in the Chesterfield Cemetery.

ALDRIDGE George Serv.# 164029

George was born on January 10th 1890 to Mr. and Mrs. David Aldridge in Plattsville. After finishing school George apprenticed as a barber and was working at his trade when he joined the army on September 6th 1915. George was 5 feet 3 inches tall. His chest when fully expanded was 35 inches with a range of expansion of 2 inches. George had a scar on his left wrist with a ruddy complexion, brown eyes and brown hair. He was considered fit for the Canadian Expeditionary Force.

ALLEN Frederick James   Serv. # 226876

Chesterfield Cenotaph

Fred was born on March 3rd 1893 to Alice and Arthur Allen at Somerton, Somerset, England. Fred was a farmer near Bright. He joined the Canadian Army in December of 1916. He was 5 feet 11 1/2 inches tall. The girth of his chest when fully expanded was 39 inches and the range of expansion was 3 1/2 inches.

Fred was killed in action on Tuesday the 1st of October 1918, while serving with the 58th Battalion of the Canadian Expeditionary Force. Fred has no known grave. His name is inscribed on the Chesterfield Cenotaph and also on the Vimy Ridge Memorial, along with the 11,284 other Canadians listed as missing and presumed dead in France during the war.

Vimy Ridge Memorial

ALLEN Jessie E.

Jessie was born to Fred and Kate Allen on October 16th 1912 in Bright.

She joined the C.W.A.C. early in the war and was posted to England in due course. She also served in Holland and sent a pair of wooden shoes from Holland to her niece Lorraine. She received her honourable discharge in late 1945. Shortly after Jessie obtained employment with Westinghouse in Toronto. She then worked at General Electric and later with Canada Wire and Cable. Jessie retired in 1977. In the 1990's Jessie moved to the Queen's Retirement Residence on Queen St. E. in Toronto.

Jessie died on March 24th 2003.

ALLEN Maurice

Maurice was born on August 28th 1910 to Fred and Kate Allen in Bright.

After finishing school Maurice worked in agriculture. In the early thirties he went to work at Canada Sand. In 1940 Maurice joined the army and served until his honourable discharge in late 1945.

Maurice went back to work at Canada Sand. He was called "Shiner" by all and sundry because of the light colour of his hair. Maurice was a quiet unassuming man, respected and well liked by all who knew him. He retired in the early 70's.

Maurice died on January 18th 1974 in his 64th year.

ALLISON Albert Wesley

Albert was born on December 7th 1904 to Robert and Isabella Allison at Washington, Ontario. After completing school he worked on the home farm and then obtained employment with Cockshutt Farm Implements in Brantford. Bert married Agnes Jane Kneller in the late thirties. Early in the war Bert joined the Royal Canadian Air Force (R.C.A.F.) and became an instrument technician. After the war he went back to Cockshutt for a while, then purchased a jewellery store in Brantford. In the 1950's Bert and his brother Roy bought Parkhaven Lake just southwest of Drumbo.

Bert died on December 27th 1979.

ANDERSON Fredrick S. Serv.# 730263

Fred was born on December 19th 1885 in Stanstead, Kent County, England. Fred, a sister and two brothers came to Canada in 1892. They were adopted by Richard Anderson and his wife who farmed in the Haysville area. After finishing his schooling he worked on his adopted father's farm.

In 1915 Fred enlisted in the 111th Battalion of the C.E.F. He was 5 feet 4 inches in height and his chest girth was 37 inches fully expanded. His range of expansion was 3 inches. Fred had a medium complexion with blue eyes and dark brown hair. He was a member of the Church of England. Fred was badly gassed at Ypres, but like many other Canadian soldiers he continued on. He returned to Canada and received his honourable discharge in 1919. Fred was granted a 20% disability pension due to the gassing he received at Ypres. This totalled $12.00 a month. Fred married Ada Soper from Kitchener on September 4th 1920. For this he was granted an additional pension of $3.00 a month. He then got a job in the furniture factory in Plattsville and he and his wife moved to Washington where another Anderson, a cousin, was running the grocery store.

Fred and Ada had three daughters. Lillian Margaret was born on July 15th 1920, Florence Catherine followed on April 9th 1922 and Hazel May completed the family on February 24th 1930. Fred always suffered from shortness of breath due to the gas but in the early 1930s he also developed heart trouble and had to quit work. The heart problem was also deemed to be due to the gas, so his pension was increased to 40% disability. With the additional for a wife and three children he received $56.00 a month.

Fred died on February 2nd 1941 and is buried in the Chesterfield cemetery.

THREE AREA GRADUATES — Kitchener and district graduates at a recent wings parade held at No. 2 Service Flying Training School at Uplands included. left to right: Sgt. A. L. Baer, Plattsville; Sgt. P. F. Jolkowski, 495 Victoria St. N., Kitchener; Sgt. D. A. Shantz, 461 Wendell Ave., Kitchener.

Ile de France steaming toward Halifax with homecoming Canadian servicemen and women, including more than 000 RCAF personnel, is greeted 180 miles off Nova Scotia coast by a Hudson aircraft, from which picture of former rench luxury liner was taken. Photographers were FO. E. K. Wells, Regina, and Sgt. C. E. Hope, Toronto.

BAER Arthur Leslie   Service # R200550

Arthur was born on August 26th 1923 to Eldon and Clara Baer. He completed Grade X11 at 16 years of age and went to work on a fruit farm near Grimsby. He joined the Air Force on November 2nd 1942. He was posted to Manning Depot in Toronto and after a stint of guard duty returned to Toronto for Initial Training School. When Churchill came to Quebec in 1943 Art was chosen as one of the Honour Guard. He took his Service Flying Training School on Harvards at Uplands near Ottawa. The Harvard was a fast single seater trainer and graduates were slated for fighter command.

Arthur went overseas in 1944 on the Queen Elizabeth and was posted to Bournemouth. After a few months he took his Operational Training Unit near Cardiff Wales on Mustangs.

After the end of the war Arthur came home on the Ile de France and received his honourable discharge on September 10th 1945. He enrolled in a machinist course in Hamilton and on completion got a job in a machine shop. He then married Noreen Catherine Burns on October 13th 1948. They had three children, Larry Arthur was born on May 13th 1949. Sharon Clair followed on December 21st 1950 and Wendy Noreen completed the family on September 2nd 1955.

Art was given the opportunity of a position at the University of Waterloo in the research and development section where he taught students the machinist trade. Students were from all different countries and Art enjoyed the challenge.

Art loved the North Country and in 1970 bought a property from the Black Watch Club of Toronto on the Sturgeon River near Waubaushene. He loved fishing, shuffle board and bridge and could indulge himself with all three at Waubaushene. Art, his wife and children converted the property into a Camp Ground which they sold in 1976. He had just got a job at R.C.A. in Midland when Mitsubishi bought R.C.A. Arthur worked there until he retired. He and his wife had a home built in Victoria Harbour. They bought a mobile trailer in a park in Florida and spent the winters in Florida and the summers in Victoria Harbour.

Arthur died on August 8th 1995.

BAIRD Addison Bell (Bud)

Bud was born on August 12th 1920 to Addison Hugh and Effie Elizabeth (nee-Bell) Baird on the family farm. After finishing school Bud worked in agriculture, both on the home farm and other farms in the area. He enlisted in the "Fighting Perths" with his brothers on September 19th 1939. The "Perths" was one of the first units to be formed and trained. In the summer of 1941 Bud fell in love with Mernie Tufgar and they were married on September 25th 1941. In October of 1941 the Regiment was shipped overseas and Bud had to leave his now pregnant wife. Their first child, Bonnie Belle, was born on June 1st 1942. In late 1943 Bud was posted back to Canada to take his Officer's Training Course. After completion of the course he was shipped back to England.

Bud was posted home in late 1945 and received his honourable discharge in early 1946. Dale Stanley was born on February 7th 1947. Shortly after Bud and Mernie bought a farm just outside of Ancaster. Two years later they had a barn fire that wiped them out. Bud then managed a Jersey farm near Caledon with show cattle. Bud specialized in Jersey cattle, and in 1951 he was hired to manage a herd in Lake Placid, New York for five years then managed a herd in Burlington, Vermont. Gregory Herbert completed the family on August 9th 1957 while they were in Burlington. Bud managed three other Jersey farms before going with the Ohio Jersey Breeders Association as editor of their magazine. The Association folded so Bud went with the Ohio Fuel and Gas Co. Mernie died on September 21st 1977. Bud retired twenty years later in 1997.

Addison Bell, always known as Bud, died on December 12th 2002.

BAIRD Andrew Oliver

Andrew was born on January 8th 1915 the second child of Addison H. and Effie E. (nee-Bell) Baird on the home farm on the Oxford/Waterloo Townline, west of County Road 22. After finishing school Andrew, like his brothers, went into agricultural work.

On September 16th 1939 he joined the Perth Regiment. He then went home and talked his brothers into joining also. They all trained in Stratford and Camp Borden and spent some time guarding the power station in Niagara Falls. He then transferred to the Royal Electrical and Mechanical Engineers and took additional training with R.E.M.E. in Hamilton.

Andrew married Jean MacKay on January 1st 1941. In October 1942 Andrew was posted overseas and a little later, on February 28th 1943 their first son Larry Alexander was born. Andrew served in France, Belgium and Holland. After the war ended Andrew was sent home and received his honourable discharge in late 1945.

Andrew worked as a mechanic and machinist before establishing his own construction company in the Dundas area. Linda Jean was born on January 19th 1948. Jeanine Kathleen followed on August 2nd 1951 and Drew Mackay completed the family on April 18th 1954.

Andrew died suddenly from a heart attack on January 15th 1966.

BAIRD John Millar

John was born on October 18th 1913 to Addison H. and Effie E. Baird on the home farm. He attended Green's School and then went to the Plattsville Continuation School. He was also a member of the reserve army with the Scots Fusiliers of Kitchener. John worked as a farm labourer until he joined the 48th Highlanders in December 1939. He was stationed in the horse palace of the C.N.E. grounds for a few days. The unit was posted overseas so John spent Christmas crossing the Atlantic. By the end of May 1940 John was in France. When the French Government capitulated he and his buddies were on a train going inland. The French crew deserted and left the train sitting on the tracks. One of the Canadian soldiers had experience with trains and took over, running them all back to Dunkirk on the English Channel where they were rescued by a flotilla of small British boats and barges.

Back in Great Britain John transferred to the Provost Corps, and spent the rest of the war years as a Military Policeman. He and another M. P. were driving in London, England during an air raid and took a direct hit from a bomb. They were both wounded, but recovered after hospitalization and some surgery. When the war ended John was shipped home and received his honourable discharge in early 1946.

John bought a farm under the Veteran's Land Act and soon after, on June 1st 1946, he married Marjorie MacIntyre. On June 2nd 1947 their first son Donald John was born. James Ralph followed on May 29th 1950 and Heather Marjorie completed the family on September 17th 1952.

John and Marjorie farmed for a while but it wasn't long before he had to give up the farm due to his wounds. He then worked for Wilmot Township and later received the job of custodian at the Baden school.

John died on January 10th 1978 in his 65th year.

BAIRD Margaret Jeanette

Margaret was born on September 2nd 1918 to Addison Hugh and Effie Elizabeth Baird on the home farm. After finishing school Margaret did housework on local farms. At the end of 1940 Margaret got a job in Hamilton at Otis Fenson factory making Bofors guns. They were an excellent anti-aircraft gun and she stayed there for two and a half years. On September 2nd 1943 Margaret left the factory and joined the R.C.A.F. Women's Division. After training in wireless at Rockliffe, near Ottawa, and also Montreal she was posted to Coastal Command in St. John's, Newfoundland. Their job was to keep in touch with the flying boats patrolling the convoys to protect them from U-boats. The flying boats had Aszdic, which helped them trace and target U-boats. Margaret received her discharge in late 1945. She worked at home for a bit and then was hired at a fruit farm near Grimsby.

On November 18th 1949 Margaret married George Alexander Penny. They farmed near Ancaster. Their first child, Margaret Elizabeth, was born on August 31st 1950. Janet Irene followed on August 3rd 1953 and Barbara Joan completed the family on October 29th 1954. They retired to a home they built on a corner of their farm near Ancaster.

In the year 2003 George is in a nursing home in Hagersville and Margaret is living in a retirement home in Caledonia. They both maintain an active interest in their family and friends.

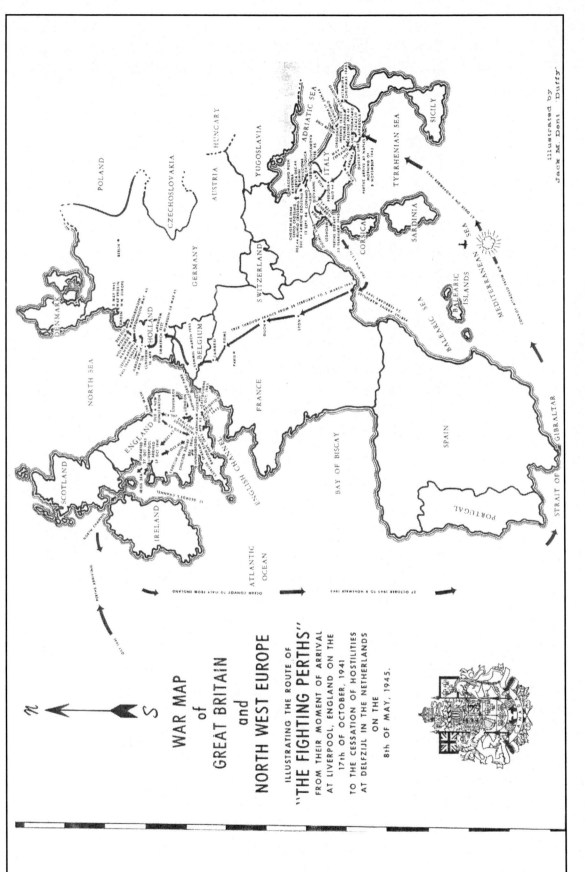

Overseas odyssey of "The Fighting Perths" and all its members.

BAIRD William David   Serv.# A-11252

Bill was born on January 23rd 1922 to Addison Hugh and Effie Elizabeth (nee-Bell) Baird. After completing his schooling he worked in agriculture both on the home farm and, during the harvest season, on neighbouring farms. He enlisted in the Perth Regiment, popularly known as "The Fighting Perths", on September 19th 1939. The war was only a couple of weeks old and Bill was one of the first in Canada to answer the call for volunteers. The Regiment was in Stratford for a short period and then posted to Camp Borden where they underwent training. The Perths were a machine gun Regiment and equipped with Vickers machine guns. In late fall they were sent to Niagara Falls to guard the Hydro Power plant. After this guard duty they had a short stint in Hamilton and then back to Borden for further training.

The Perth Regiment went overseas in October 1941. They disembarked at Liverpool on October 17th 1941 and were taken to Chilton Foliat for military exercises till April 1942 when they were posted to Farnham in Surrey for further training. In July 1942 the Perths were on the move again to Aldershot. In December 1942 they were sent to the Brighton Hove area for a battle course. They received more specialized training at Barton Stacey and Eastbourne before shipping out from Liverpool on October 27th 1943 for Italy. They were attacked by enemy aircraft south of Sardinia in the Mediterranean. The Perths arrived at Naples on November 8th 1943. They fought their way up Italy from Monte Cassino to the Senio Crossing by Christmas 1944. They had to fight through the Gustav Line, the Hitler Line and the Gothic Line. Every stream and hill was fortified and had to be attacked. It was brutal fighting all the way as the terrain suited the defenders. After a year of constant fighting the Perths finally completed their work in Italy and shipped out of Florence on the 22nd of February 1945 arriving in Marseilles in their Landing Ship Tanks two days later. Bill didn't like Italy, although he did like the wine. They then trekked through France from 28th of February to the 5th of March, passing through Lyon, Dijon, Reims and Cambrai to Kemmel in Belgium. They fought their way through Belgium and Holland taking Nijmegen on the 28th of March and then up through Arnhem, Groningen to Defzijl where hostilities ended on the 8th of May 1945.

Bill volunteered for the Pacific and was shipped home early. "Victory in Japan" day came shortly after so he received his honourable discharge on September 26th 1945. On August 26th 1946 he married Edna Mae Rennick. In the fall of 1946 he bought the International Farm Implement agency in Bright. He also ran a gravel truck and went into well drilling.

He and Edna had four children. John David was born on December 28th 1946. Douglas William followed on September 15th 1948. They then had two daughters, Judith Patricia arrived on March 21st 1954 and Linda Lee on October 4th 1955. Edna Mae died on January 7th 1993 and is sadly missed.

Bill, in 2003, is retired and lives in Bright.

BAKER Roy Carman Serv. # V 70579

Roy was born on February 11th 1925 to Charles and Lisa Baker of Chesterfield. The lot that the Chesterfield church is built on was originally part of their farm. After finishing school Roy worked in agriculture until he joined the Royal Canadian Navy on September 8th 1942. He joined up in London, Ontario, and was immediately posted to Montcalm Quebec for six weeks initial training. His next posting was to H.M.C.S Cornwallis near Digby Nova Scotia where he was trained as a gunner. After successful completion of his course Roy was assigned to the H.M.C.S. Matapedia, a Corvette armed with two 4 inch guns and two 40 mm. Oerilkon guns. Naturally they also carried between 50 and 100 depth charges. They had a complement of roughly 80 men. The Corvette was like a small destroyer and tossed around like a cork in a rough sea. The Matapedia was on convoy duty. They would take a convoy from Halifax to St. Johns, Newfoundland, then half way across the Atlantic. They would meet a convoy coming back and escort them to New York. Then back to Halifax to begin the round again. Roy received his honourable discharge on January 20th 1946 and was awarded the Canadian Volunteer Service Medal and Clasp and the War Medal 1939-45. He should also be entitled to the Atlantic star and has applied for consideration.

He worked on his brother's farm till early 1949 when he went with Davidson & McGinnis Hardware in Woodstock and learned the sheet metal trade.

On February 25th 1950 Roy married Annie Louise Barnett. They had three children. Dennis Carman was born on September 28th 1950. Terry Roy followed on February 12th 1952 and Nancy Louise completed the family on November 25th 1957.

In 1967 Roy bought the R.C. Cowan Hardware and Sheet Metal in Drumbo. He sold the business to his son Dennis in 1987 and worked at the store till 1990 when Roy finally retired. Dennis sold the store but has continued in the sheet metal business.

Roy died suddenly on February 3rd 2004.

BARRETT Albert Sydney   Serv.# R89482

Bert was born on November 17th 1918 to Frederick and Rhoda Mae Barrett in Plattsville. He was named after two brothers of his father who were killed in the First World War. He enlisted in August 1940 in the R.C.A.F. He attended the Galt Aircraft School for 6 months, then was stationed in Toronto and St. Thomas. He was honourably discharged June 1941 for medical reasons.

Bert had started working for Canada Sand in 1935 and was taken back upon his discharge from the air force. On July 28th 1951 he married Edythe Pearl Percy. They had four children, Kent Robert born August 29th 1952, Ruth Anne Marie followed on March 9th 1954. Janice Jean was next on April 10th 1955 and the family was completed with Elaine Louise on May 17th 1956.

Bert died on July 21st 1992.

BATTLER Nile Earl

Nile was born on March 16th 1922 to George Wesley and Ida Battler on the family farm south of Washington. Nile worked on the home farm after completing High School in Plattsville. He joined the army in late 1940 and shortly after his father sold the farm to the Community Farm of the Brethren. After suitable training Nile was transferred to the Elgin Regiment. They were an Armoured Delivery Regiment and Nile was one of their drivers. They handled Stag Hounds, Sherman Tanks and Bren Gun Carriers. They waterproofed these units and made sure they were in top shape before delivering them. The regiment went over to France right after the invasion and did their maintenance work and delivery all through France, Belgium, Holland and into Germany. Nile was very calm and measured in his response to events. He never lost his temper regardless of provocation. The unit and Nile were returned to Canada in October 1945. Shortly after he received his honourable discharge.

After the war Nile got a job as a bus driver for the P.U.C. in Kitchener. He met and wooed a charming young lady and on December 3rd 1947 he married Wilhelmine Margaret Foerster. Nile

often said it was the smartest thing he ever did. They had a daughter, Dienne Brenda, on April 2nd 1951. After driving for a few years Nile joined the Kitchener Hydro as a meter reader. In due course he was promoted to supervisor. He retired at 65 years of age in 1987.

Nile died on April 9th 1993.

BELL George Scott   Serv.# A56500

George was born on May 5th 1915 in Plattsville to David Harkness Bell and his wife Mary Jane. After he finished school he did agricultural work on dairy farms. On the 28th of January 1940 he enlisted in the Royal Canadian Ordinance Corps. George served in Canada, the U.K., France and Belgium. He received his honourable discharge on December 6th 1945. George did 1774 days of service with 1441 of those days overseas.

He received the Canadian Volunteer Service Medal and Clasp, the France Germany Star and the War Medal 1939-45.

On coming home he worked for a short time at Bairds Machine Shop in Woodstock. He and his brother then ran a gravel business in Bright and expanded to the feed business. Later he also sold electric welders.

On June 28th 1947 George married Margaret Ethel Kell from Simcoe County. They had five children, James Ronald on August 7th 1948, Ross Seymour on March 15th 1951, a daughter Patricia Jean came on March 17th 1955 followed by Catherine Margaret on August 23rd 1956. The last child was a son, Bruce George, born on August the 18th 1965.

George died on November 14th 1969.

BELL Robert Davis

Bob was born on March 20th 1913 in Plattsville to David Harkness Bell and his wife, Mary Jane. After graduating from school he did agricultural work in the area. He went overseas in the army. After the war he went to Saskatchewan and worked for the Federal Government in Plant Operations.

In 1961 Bob married Rose Hardy.

Robert

BERGEY Douglas Willard Service # B72283

Doug was born in Washington, Ontario on December 4th 1921 to Willard and Effie Mae Bergey. He married Marion Cane on May 31st 1941. They had a son, Robert Wayne, born on February 12th 1942. Doug was working at the Alabastine Plant in Paris, but left to join the army in October 1942 as a private in the Army Medical Corps. He was stationed in Toronto, Brampton and Camp Borden for training. On February 3rd 1943 Doug and Marion had a daughter Beverly Jean. In March 1943 he sailed for England but was only there three weeks when he was posted to North Africa. He was shipped to Sicily for the invasion and then on to Italy. At this time Doug was a stretcher bearer, often an unpleasant and dangerous type of work. From Italy he went to France shortly after D-Day. Doug also drove ambulance and in due course he served in Belgium, Holland and Germany. He was in Holland when the war ended.

In December 1945 Doug came home on the Queen Elizabeth, the largest ship afloat. Shortly after he received his honourable discharge and went back to his old job in Paris. He then bought a farm under the Veteran's Land Act just outside Burgessville. On March 30th 1947 Marilyn Joy was born and another sister, Gloria Grace, came along on December 31st 1952.

In 1955 Doug was offered a Dealership for Surge milking machines in Embro and decided to take it. In Embro the last daughter was born, Glenda Darlene on May 3rd 1958. In 1967 Doug went to Ottawa, still in the dairy business.

Doug died on August 8th 1969.

BERST George Elmer

George was born in 1897 to Adam and Elizabeth Berst in Plattsville. George joined up in 1915 and wound up training for the Royal Flying Corps. In 1919 George married Jessie Pearl Hewitt of Bright. He was discharged from the forces in 1920. George became a teacher and started his career at the Windfall school. He then obtained a position in Woodstock and spent most of his career in Woodstock schools.

Their first son, Alfred Hewitt, was born on August 8th 1920. Alfred followed in his father's footsteps and became a Flying Officer with the Royal Canadian Air Force (R.C.A.F.) in the Second World War. Norma Elizabeth followed on November 25th 1924. Margaret Pearl joined the family on January 7th 1932 closely followed by Imogene Barbara on February 20th 1933. John Ward, who became Principal of the Plattsville & District Public School, completed the family on November 24th 1935.

George died on May 11th 1966.

BLACKMORE Harvey Lloyd Service # R118691

Harvey was born on June 10th 1920 in Plattsville to Reginald Thomas and Lea Marie Blackmore. In 1936 he started to work at Canada Sand. On July 14th 1941 he joined the Air Force and trained as an aero engine mechanic with the rank of L.A.C. He was stationed in Winnipeg, St. Thomas and Brandon. He was posted to Dartmouth, Nova Scotia where he met his future wife. After some time he was posted to Quebec and then back to Nova Scotia. He wanted to marry Miss Boudreau in his home town when he was posted back to Ontario. In June 1945 Harvey's wish came true and he married Florence Boudreau in Plattsville. Harvey volunteered for the Pacific but Victory in Japan (V.J.) Day scotched that so he was discharged on September 27th 1945.

Harvey went back to work at Canada Sand. In 1947 their first child, Cheryl Ann was born. She was very sick and tragically died two days later. On September 5th 1948 their only son, Donald James, was born. He was followed by twins, Ruth Eleanor and Louise Mary, born on December 20th 1949. On July 8th 1953 Lynn Marie arrived followed by Merrilee on May 29th 1955. The last child was Wendy Joan who was born on August 22nd 1956. On March 13th 1959 Florence died, leaving a very young family.

On June 12th 1959 Harvey married Myrna Dolores Crawford. For the next 20 years he continued working at Canada Sand, retiring after 40 years service in 1979. Harvey continued to enjoy life and his family. He died on July 13th 2001 at 81 years of age.

BLACKMORE Reginald Thomas   Serv.# 388474

Tom was born to George and Mary Ann Blackmore in 1891 in London, England. They emigrated to Canada in 1895 and settled in Toronto. After finishing school he found employment delivering bread. Some time later he obtained employment with the Canadian National Railway and wound up in Parry Sound where he met Leah Dubie and wed her on May 5th 1913. On September 22nd 1914 Eleanor was born followed by two babies, Bernice and Reginald. Tragically they both died as babies.

On April 1st 1915 Reg joined the Canadian Army Service Corps in Toronto, Ontario. He was 5' 7" tall, of medium complexion, with blue eyes and dark brown hair. He had a Crucifix tattooed on his left breast and an anchor on his left arm. He served in France and was gassed, which affected his health in future years. He received his honourable discharge on August 7th 1919. A son Harvey Lloyd was born on June 10th 1920. Roy Joseph followed on July 2nd 1923 with Ronald Thomas appearing on August 8th 1928. Mary Ann completed the family on January 21st 1937.

After the war Reg and his family settled in Toronto where he worked for a firm making small aluminum utensils and tools. He joined the Legion and spent much time on Legion work. His health deteriorated so in 1937 they moved to Plattsville. He obtained employment at Canada Sand and pumped gas at the McKie Gas Pumps. After a year or so Reg started a shoe repair business. The business went well and he worked at it till his death on September 15th 1965.

BLACKMORE Ronald Thomas

Ron was born on August 8th 1928 to Reginald Thomas and Lea Marie Blackmore. On October 5th 1944 he joined the army as a Private in the Canadian Army Technical Training Corps in Hamilton. On September 18th 1945 he was released from the army because he was under 18 years of age. On September 22nd 1947 he re-enlisted in the permanent force and was posted to Picton, Ontario for training in the Royal Canadian School of Anti-Aircraft artillery.

On July 31st 1948 Ron married Mildred Grace Milner. They had three children, Leah Marie was born on February 20th 1949, Ralph Edward appeared on March 18th 1950, then Nancy Louise completed the family on February 14th 1955.

In 1952 Ron was posted to Portage La Prairie, Manitoba training militia troops. In 1954 he was promoted to Sergeant. He then spent time at Rivers, Manitoba taking parachute training and received his Paratrooper wings. His next posting was a tour of duty for one year in Churchill, Manitoba where he was fortunate enough to see some polar bears at fairly close range. A three year stint in Edmonton followed, again training the local militia and then a year at Carp on the early warning centre.

Ron was posted to Petawawa for the worst four years of his life. It was bad for him, bad for his children and bad for his wife. His experience and abilities were then recognized as more valuable for National Defence Headquarters. On October 22nd 1971, after eight years in Ottawa, Ron retired.

Ron   Harvey   Roy

BLACKMORE Roy Joseph John   Serv.# A 82124

Roy was born to Reginald Thomas and Lea Marie on July 2nd 1923. He enlisted in the Oxford Rifles on April 27th 1942 and then spent the next three years and four months as a private in the army. He went to London, Ontario where Ed Fergusson (another Plattsville man) was forming a unit which was then posted to Prince George, British Columbia for training. In September 1942 a draft of 194 soldiers of the Oxford Rifles was sent to London, Ontario and given three days embarkation leave. This was highly unusual as the minimum was supposed to be two weeks. They were then sent by train to Halifax and embarked on the SS Sterling Castle. Alvin Fulcher, another Plattsville man, was also on board.

They landed in Liverpool at the beginning of October, and were sent to a holding unit. There Roy volunteered to join the Essex Scottish Regiment. They were sent to France at the end of June and got into the thick of the action around Caen. A little over a month later, on July 11th 1944 he was wounded in the chest by shrapnel from a mortar shell. He still has several pieces of shrapnel in his chest. He was soon back in action again near Caen. While taking cover in a fox hole from German artillery Hudson Chambers, a friend from Bright, jumped in and joined him. He was wounded again on the 21st of July. This time a tank shell got him in the shoulder, buttocks, and back of his legs and he had to be hospitalized for a much longer period. This wound has left shrapnel in his legs. Roy was wounded for the third time on January 21st 1945. The unit was attacking in Germany and Roy was hit in the left shoulder by two Schmeisser bullets. The Schmeisser was similar to our Sten and Tommy guns, but quite a bit better. Roy was hospitalized and operated on in Holland and then sent by ambulance to England and hospitalized for a further three months. On April 23rd 1945 Roy came home on the SS Lady Nelson. He was again hospitalized in Westminster Hospital in London for the best part of six weeks. He received his discharge on June 6th 1945.

On March 2nd 1946 Roy married Betty Barbara Brown. They had eight children, Barbara on March 15th 1947. Murray John, a brother, showed up on August 21st 1948. Richard David weighed in on November 23rd 1949. Joann Marie joined the family on August 21st 1948 followed by Marlane Joy on June 30th 1953. The last three were all boys, Roy Allen on June 27th 1954, Budd Edward on August 14th 1957 and last but not least Lawrence Scott on June 24th 1962.

Roy and Betty have enjoyed every minute of their family life. They now have over 22 grandchildren and 28 great grandchildren. Betty unfortunately died on August 13th 2003. Roy spent most of his working life in Woodstock so still resides there amongst friends and relatives.

Precious Moments

I dreamed of you the other day,
You were standing by my side.
As you always did so many years,
That it almost made me cry.

You told me things that life would hold,
And the many things I'd see.
The heart aches and the happiness,
That would someday come to me.

Now you are no longer here with me,
To tell me what life's about.
Of trial and tribulations,
Of this world so full of doubt.

As I stand before your monument,
With these memories from my mind.
Let me thank you for these moments,
And the pictures of our time.

Roy J.J. Blackmore

BOURNE Allan William   Serv. # B-134825

Allan was born on April 9th 1923 in Washington, Ontario to Harry and Maude Bourne. After finishing school he did agricultural work. In 1942 he enlisted in the Toronto Scottish Regiment. He was stationed in Toronto, Brantford and Camp Borden for infantry training. Allan was posted to England in February 1943 where he received further training. His unit was involved in D Day and then fought through France, Belgium, Holland and Germany. Allan was transferred to the Lorne Scots while in France. He was in hospital with head injuries at the end of the war.

Allan married May Kerr from Dundee, Scotland on January 25th 1946. They had 5 children. Bonnita Ellen was the first, born on March 20th 1948, Ian James followed on July 19th 1949. Steven arrived on June 28th 1951 and a sister, Doris Mary, joined the clan on May 24th 1952. Deborah Anne completed the family on October 21st 1960.

Allan died on October 31st 1994 in Windsor, Ontario.

BRANSCOMBE Frederic Ray

Frederic was born on June 4th 1914 in Moncton, New Brunswick to Arthur D. and Ada (nee-Lutes) Branscombe. The family moved to Toronto and after finishing school Fred went to the University of Toronto and earned his Honours B.A. in English and History. He then attended Teachers College in Toronto as a specialist in English and History. From 1939 to 1942 he taught at the Plattsville Continuation School. In July 1942 Fred joined the Army and was in the infantry. His medical condition limited his usefulness in the physical side of operations however his education made him extremely valuable in the intelligence area. He was posted to Ottawa and shortly after was promoted to 2nd Lieutenant. Fred was promoted to Captain in due course. He received his honourable discharge in February of 1946.

Frederic obtained employment at the Secondary School in Grimsby. He then married Dorothy Margaret Raggatt on June 29th 1946. Dorothy and Frederic had twin daughters, Ellen Louise and Margaret Dorothy born on April 18th 1950. In 1962 Ed took his Masters Degree in Educational Communications at New York University. In 1970 he obtained his Ph.D. at New York University. in the same field. He went from Grimsby to Weston Collegiate Institute and then to North York where he was the Co-ordinator of Audio-Visual Aids.

After a rewarding career in teaching Frederic retired to Toronto in the mid 1970's. In 2003 he and Dorothy are still active in community activities and enjoy life.

BRICKER Oliver Clayton

Oliver was born on December 29th 1898 to Mr. and Mrs. O.S. Bricker in Elgin, Manitoba. The family moved to Plattsville, Ontario shortly after where Oliver took his education. On the 15th of June 1917 Oliver joined the 108th Regiment of the Canadian Expeditionary Force (C.E.F.). On August 25th 1917 he was transferred from the 108th Regiment to the No. 1 Special Service Company. Oliver was 5 feet 6 inches tall. His chest girth when fully expanded was 34 1/2 inches and his range of expansion was 3 1/2 inches. Oliver had a fair complexion with grey eyes and fair hair. He was a member of the United Brethren denomination.

This picture was taken with a group of veterans in Plattsville on August the 11th 1919. Oliver received his honourable discharge shortly after.

BRIGHTY John Robert   Service # A 82006

John was born on September 4th 1916 in Meadowvale. The family soon moved to Preston. John delivered papers and one of his customers was P.R. Hilborn, who had financed Canada Sand. When he finished school John asked P.R. if he could get him a job. P.R. did just that at Canada Sand in Plattsville. In June of 1940 John joined the local militia unit, the Oxford Rifles. On August 17th 1940 John married Beatrice May Barrett. He enlisted in the regular army on March 31st 1942. He was stationed at London and Camp Borden where he took his Sergeant's course then on to Prince George for further training. While there he received word his daughter Norma Mae had been born on September 10th 1942. He was posted overseas in February of 1943 for 13 months and promoted to Sergeant-Major while attached to the Royal Canadian Regiment. He was sent home for a Commission at Brockville and was promoted to Lieutenant in July 1944. He returned overseas in March 1945, and in due course was promoted to Captain.

After his discharge John rejoined Canada Sand. On October 26th 1946 a son, Paul Barrett, was born to John and Beatrice. Carborundum Abrasives bought Canada Sand and in 1961 sent John to their plant in Niagara Falls, New York to head up production planning. John and Beatrice elected to live in Niagara Falls, Ontario. He retired in 1979 and they continued to live in Niagara Falls.

John died on May 24th 1997.

BRISTOW Douglas Edward Serv. # 164036

Douglas was born in Bright on September 8th 1897. His father was James E. Bristow. Doug joined the army on August 29th 1915. He was 5 feet 7 1/2 inches tall and the girth of his chest when fully expanded was 34 1/2 inches. His attestation papers show him as of fair complexion, hazel eyes and fair hair with a scar over his right eye. His religious denomination was Presbyterian.

Doug was attached to the 84th Battalion at Niagara Camp on September 6th 1915. After due training he was posted overseas and became a Sergeant with the 75th Battalion of the Canadian Expeditionary Force. On the 30th of September 1918 he was missing in action and like so many other soldiers in the First World War, has no known grave.

His name is inscribed on the Vimy Ridge Memorial and the Cenotaph in the Chesterfield church yard.

BROWN Clifford   Serv. # 204537

Tyne Cot Cemetery

Chesterfield Cenotaph

Cliff was born on the 19th of July 1898. His father was Ralph Brown of Plattsville with a farm near Ratho. He enlisted in the army on March 23rd 1916 in Saskatoon Sask. as he was working on a Farm near Zealandia. Cliff was 5 feet 7 inches tall and the girth of his chest when fully expanded was 35 1/2 inches with a range of expansion of 3 1/2 inches. His complexion was fresh, his eyes grey and his hair dark. He was a Presbyterian.

Clifford was killed on the 2nd of November 1917 while serving with the 42nd Battalion of the Canadian Black Watch as a private. His name is inscribed on the Cenotaph at Chesterfield and he is buried in the Tyne Cot Cemetery # 125 at Passchendaele in Belgium.

The small battlefield cemetery near Tyne Cot was expanded after the war and became the largest British Military Cemetery. There are 11,962 headstones and 34,888 names of the dead with no known grave are commemorated on the rear walls.

BROWN David Armstrong   Serv.# R183743

David Brown was born on May 11th 1924 to Walter H. and Olive Lois Brown above the family hardware store in Bright. After completing Grade X in 1940 David left school, moved to Woodstock and went to work for LaFrance Textiles until he was old enough to enlist in the air force. On August 22nd 1942 David enlisted in the Royal Canadian Air Force (R.C.A.F.) and was posted to Brandon Manitoba for Manning Depot and then to Initial Training School. On completion he was posted to Calgary for Wireless Training and qualified as a Wireless Operator on July 19th 1943. Dave was then posted to No. 1 Bombing and Gunnery School in Jarvis, Ontario. He started his course on July 26th and graduated on September 6th 1943 as a Wireless Air Gunner. He then flew in Ansons out of Summerside, P.E.I. until July 18th 1944 when he was posted to #1 Y Depot in Lachine Quebec. On August 29th 1944 he embarked on the S.S. Acquitania for Britain and arrived on September 5th and was then sent to the #3 Personnel Reception Centre in Bournemouth. In December David was sent to # 10 R.S. at the Royal Air Force (R.A.F.) station at Carew Cheriton in South Wales. On the 28th of February 1945 he was posted to #6 Operational Training Unit in Silloth, Cumberland where he was teamed up with a crew. They completed their training on Wellington Bombers and at the end of May were posted to # 407 R.C.A.F. Squadron at Chivenor, North Devon. As the war had ended David was shipped home and received his honourable discharge on September 22nd 1945. He had logged 781 hours and 50 minutes of flying time. He never flew again.

After his discharge he worked for Shell Industries in Woodstock making concrete blocks. In 1946 he apprenticed as a plumber to Davidson McGinnis Hardware. He married Pauline Bier on October 19th 1946. In 1949 David started Dave Brown Plumbing and Heating. He and Pauline had three children. Robert John was born on July 13th 1955, Katherine Ann followed on March 22nd 1959 and Kenneth Davis completed the family on December 18th 1960. In 1983 David and Pauline divorced. David retired in 1988. He was an avid hunter and fisherman. He also enjoyed curling and was a very competent lawn bowler.

David died of cancer on March 7th 1993.

BROWN Douglas Landseer

Plattsville Memorial Gates

Douglas was born on July 27th 1890 to Mr. and Mrs. J.L. Brown in Plattsville, Ontario. After completing school Doug went into dentistry and when he received his Doctorate, set up practice in Winnipeg. He joined the Canadian Army Dental Corps with the rank of Captain on August 20th 1917.

BROWN George Norval Murray

Norval was born on January 12th 1909. After finishing school Norval worked in agriculture and went on two harvest excursions to Saskatchewan. There he met Marion Jane Honey from Riverhurst, Saskatchewan. They were married on August 8th 1928. After Canada Sand opened he was employed with them. The first child, Betty Barbara was born on May 14th 1929; Robert George followed on May 30th 1936; then came Hedley James on April 17th 1938. Melvin Kenneth completed the family on June 28th, 1940.

Norval joined the army in January 1941. He served overseas in the Transport Division of the Artillery. He came home in late 1944 and was discharged in January 1945. He then went to work at Lochman's Garage in Plattsville. Shortly after he bought a farm under the Veteran's Land Act on the 12th Concession. Some time later a restaurant became available in Bright, so Norval sold the farm and bought the restaurant and a house in Bright. He and his wife ran it very successfully until his death on January 18th 1979.

BROWN Glen Wilson

Glen was born on January 28th 1927 in Plattsville. He enlisted in the Canadian Army on October 16th 1944 and was posted to the Technical School studying Mechanics and Electricity. He was later transferred to the Driving and Maintenance school in Woodstock. He volunteered for the Pacific but the Atom Bomb convinced the Japanese to surrender. As a result Glen took his discharge shortly after and worked in a factory for a year.

He preferred the army life so re-enlisted in 1948. He went into Royal Electrical & Mechanical Engineers (R.E.M.E.) and was posted to Shilo, a big army base in Manitoba. While in Shilo he met Eireene Myrtle Ehlin who lived in Brandon. The romance flourished and they were married on February 27th 1952. They had four children.

Catherine Yvonne was born on November 22nd 1952, Constance Ann followed on August 4th 1955. Richard Glen, the lone boy, was born on December 17th 1958. Kimberly Dawn completed the family on June 13th 1961.

All Glen's service time was spent in Canada except for the best part of a year in 1957-8 when he was stationed in Virginia taking an aircraft technicians course.

Glen was always interested in sports, playing both hockey and baseball and coaching various little league teams in those sports. He also loved fishing.

Glen retired from the army on September 29th 1973 and he and Eireene moved to Vernon, British Columbia.

Glen died on March 11th 1979.

BROWN Jack Gilbert

Jack was born on December 7th 1931 to Frank and Anne Brown in Riverhurst, Saskatchewan. They moved to Plattsville in 1934 and Frank obtained employment at Canada Sand. After finishing school in 1947 Jack was hired at Canada Sand. In January 1951 he joined the Canadian Army and was posted to Petawawa in Ontario for training. He joined the First Battalion of the Royal Canadian Regiment and they were then shipped to Wainwright, Alberta for more training. In December of 1951 they were shipped out from Seattle, Washington for a tour of duty in Korea. Jack spent two leaves of seven days in Tokyo and on one leave ran into Fred Sinclair. It was a welcome change from the combat in Korea. In May 1953 Jack left Korea and returned to Canada. In July 1953 he was posted to Rivers, Manitoba for training as a paratrooper. After successfully completing that course he was posted to Kingston where he received his honourable discharge in January of 1954.

Jack returned to Plattsville and was rehired at Canada Sand. After some time he took up plumbing. On August 2nd 1957 Jack married Helen Lena Vandelinde. They then moved to Norwich, where they have resided ever since. On May 9th 1958 a daughter, Dawn Christine was born. Twins followed, Wendy Agnes and Wanda Adriana were born on January 14th 1965. Cynthia Jane followed on December 11th 1966 and Jacqueline joined the family on July 11th 1970. Sandra Elizabeth came on July 27th 1973 with Patricia joining on June 23rd 1975. The lone boy, James Keith, was born on June 6th 1979.

In 1958 Jack was involved in a very bad automobile accident and has been on compensation ever since.

BROWN William Frank

Bill was born on December 24th 1926 to Frank and Agnes (nee Jones) Brown in Plattsville. After finishing school Bill joined the army in the spring of 1944. He received his honourable discharge in September of 1945. Bill then went to work for Sherk Transport and then went with V.J. Kaufman. In 1948 Bill was hired by Canada Sand and stayed with them until he retired in 1990.

On October 2nd 1948 Bill married Jean Main. Heather Jean started the family on April 11th 1949 followed by Brenda Lee on December 25th 1951. James Lionel arrived on December 21st 1952 with Deborah Ann, the last daughter, coming on January 21st 1954. Barton Bradley completed the family on February 23rd 1959.

Bill and Jean, in March 2004, still enjoy their house in Plattsville.

BROWN Louis Taylor Serv.# 3310039

Plattsville Memorial Gates

Louis was born on March 26th 1897 to Alexander and Mary (nee Fenn) Brown in Drumbo, Ontario. The family moved to Plattsville shortly after. Louis joined the army on September 26th 1917 with an A-2 category. Louis was 5 feet 5 1/2 inches tall. His chest was 32 inches and when fully expanded 35 inches. He had a medium complexion with brown eyes and dark hair.

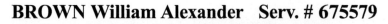

BROWN William Alexander   Serv. # 675579

Chesterfield Cenotaph

William was born in Plattsville on May 3rd 1895. He was the son of Alexander and Mary Brown (nee-Fenn). Bill enlisted in the 168th Battalion on February 19th 1916. He was 5 feet 8 inches tall with a chest girth of 37 inches when fully expanded, the range of expansion was 5 inches. He was of dark complexion with brown eyes and black hair. He was a member of the Presbyterian church. William was serving in France with the 21st Battalion of the Canadian Expeditionary Force (C.E.F) as a Private when he was badly wounded. He died of his wounds at No. 7 Casualty Clearing Centre on the 15th of August 1917 at the age of 22 years. William's name is engraved on the Cenotaph at Chesterfield and he is buried in the Ligny St. Flochel British Cemetery at Averdoingt, France # 14. The cemetery was started at the beginning of April 1918 when the 7th Casualty Clearing Station came back from Tincques ahead of the German advance. There are now 632 Commonwealth burials of the First World War in this cemetery and a further 46 German war graves. The cemetery was designed by Sir Reginald Blomfield.

BROWN William James Serv # 3135200

Bill was born on November 15th 1896 to Mr. and Mrs. Franklin Brown of R.R. #4 Blenheim, Ontario. After completing school he went into agricultural work on the family farm. On May 14th 1918 Bill joined the Canadian Expeditionary Force (C.E.F.). He was 5 feet 8 inches tall and his chest girth was 38 1/2 inches when fully expanded. The range of expansion was 3 inches. Bill was a member of the Anglican Church. This picture of Bill was taken on August 11th 1919 in Plattsville.

CHAMBERS Hubert Hudson

Hudson was born on September 1st 1924 to Edward and Sarah Maude Chambers. He joined the Highland Light Infantry on December 6th 1941. (Hudson lied about his age.) He spent the next two months in the army barracks in Kitchener. The next stop was Listowel for two months infantry training. Ipperwash took up another three months and then on to DeBert, Nova Scotia for a further four months training. After an embarkation leave Hudson was shipped overseas on the Mauretania and landed in Liverpool in December 1942 and was sent to Aldershot with the rest of the army draft.

While there he was posted to the Lincoln and Welland Regiment who came from Niagara Falls. At the end of 1943 Hudson had a hernia operation and when he recovered was posted to the Essex Scottish. Canadians received extensive training in England and some of that training was near Tunbridge Wells. A favourite watering hole was the Boars Head Pub in Farnborough. Three days after the invasion he landed in France with the Essex Scottish. In heavy fighting around Caen, Hudson was forced to take cover from a German artillery barrage and jumped into a fox hole on top of Roy Blackmore, a surprise to them both. On July 27th 1944 Hudson was taken prisoner at the Falaise Gap. There were 82 captured with him at Falaise, many of them were badly wounded. Out of the 82 only 17 got back. He was taken to Stalag 8B in Poland for the duration of the war. Stalag 8B was at Hindenburgh on the Oder River. It was at the corner where Poland, Czechoslovakia and Germany meet. Hudson was put to work in the coal mines on maintenance. The belts used in the mine were a good meter in width. There were British, South African, Australian and New Zealand prisoners in the camp. Most of the underground work was done by Russian prisoners. In December the Russians were getting too close, so the prisoners were marched out in groups of 500. It was bloody cold, but they didn't have winter clothing. Hudson's toes were frozen and many prisoners dropped by the way. They were liberated on April 24th 1945 by the Americans 14 km from Vienna. The Americans flew them to Rhiems in France. At this time Hudson weighed 92 lbs. The Americans kept him in their hospital to fix up his feet and put a little fat on his ribs for the next three weeks. He just got to Aldershot in time for the riots and was then flown to a convalescent home in Scotland. He stayed there until July. On July 8th 1945 he left for Canada on the Queen Mary, arriving in New York on July 12th. They disembarked and took a train to London, Ontario arriving at 6:00 P.M. Hudson was discharged on August 29th 1945.

Hudson went to work at York Knitting Mills in Woodstock for four months and he then went into construction and was very successful. For a while he and Harry Goff worked together. Hudson retired 41 years later. On September 24th 1947 Hudson married Nellie Marion Lamour from Tillsonburg. They had four children, Elizabeth Jean was born on November 19th 1953, Mark Edmond on July 1st 1956. Douglas Paul came on July 31st 1959 and Kenneth Hudson was the last on March 28th 1963. Nellie died on December 25th 1983. On August 25th 1985 Hudson married Gay Melba Clark. In 2003 they still reside in Woodstock.

CHRISTENSEN Erna Geraldine

Erna was born on March 26th 1925 in Plattsville. She joined the Canadian Womens Army Corps as a private in 1944 in London and received her basic training in Kitchener. She took her driver training in Woodstock and then was posted to Toronto. She worked on the Lake Shore for a year, mainly in the mechanical field. She was in the army for a little better than a year when the war ended.

After Erna received her honourable discharge she went down to New Brunswick and enrolled in a hair dressing course. She met Charles Ferguson and married him on December 21st 1946. They lived in St. John for 21 years. She and Charles had three children. Wayne was born on July 1st 1948, Greg arrived on August 10th 1949, and Susan, the last child, was born on November 21st 1951. The family moved to Ontario in 1965 and settled in Mississauga where she and her family lived. Charles died in August 1983. Erna lived on in Mississauga until her death on August 31st 1993 at 68 years of age.

CHRISTENSEN Henry Drachmann

Henry was born on May 31st, 1899. He emigrated from Denmark in 1916. He married Melissa Mae Kenyon in 1917 and enlisted at Wolsey Barracks in London, Ontario shortly after.

Henry and Melissa had five children. Dorothy Irene was born on February 20th 1919. Alice May followed on June 13th 1920, then came Mary Lydia on January 6th 1922. Russell Henry was the first boy born on August 1st 1923, Erna Geraldine followed on March 26th 1925. Melissa died tragically in September 1928. Edna Zehr assisted in bringing up the children and in early 1932 Henry and Edna were married. They had four children. Audrey Eileen was born on March 29th 1932. Elizabeth Harriet came on September 8th 1934 and was followed by Richard Drachmann on May 11th 1936. Katharine Joan was the last child on July 26th 1939.

After the First World War Henry worked for Ivan Hall at Perry's Corners for a few years. He then worked for Dr. Nurse and also delivered bread. When Canada Sand was opened in 1930 Henry was hired as a stationary engineer. He worked at Canada Sand until his death on August 7th 1964. Henry was a very kind and gentle man.

CHRISTENSEN Jens

Jens emigrated to Canada in 1916 with his brother Henry. He enlisted with his brother in 1917 and they both came home and received their honourable discharges in 1919. There is no information available as to where he went after the war.

CHRISTENSEN Russell Henry   Service No. A105058

Russell was born on August 1st 1923 to Henry and Melissa in Blenheim Township. After finishing school he worked as a labourer and turned his hand to any work that was available. He was fortunate and obtained a job at Shurly-Dietrich-Atkins in Galt. His father came from Denmark. Russ enlisted in the Canadian Army on October 29th 1942. He had been with the Highland Light Infantry, a militia unit in Galt and was recruited as a Corporal. He was stationed at Listowel, Camp Borden and Ipperwash.

He was posted overseas in March 1943. After a year in England he joined the Algonquin Regiment. His Regiment went to France and Belgium. He was wounded on September 17th 1944. He was taken prisoner at the Leopold Canal. His parents were notified he was missing and only found he had survived when Russell's voice was heard over a short wave radio broadcast from a prison camp in Germany. Shortly after he was transferred to a camp in Poland. The Russians got too close so the Germans, on February 8th 1945, marched the prisoners to the west. They went roughly 15 miles a day and marched 600 miles in 35 days. They wound up in a prison camp at Bad-Orb, were liberated by the Americans and flown to England. As soon as he arrived in England he cabled his parents to let them know his whereabouts. Conditions and food in the prison camp had not been good. He arrived home in May 1945 and was sent to a Sanatorium for a year to treat a very bad case of pleurisy. Russ received his honourable discharge in 1946.

When he was released he went to Toronto to take a watch making course. When the course was completed he moved to Stratford where he worked in a jewellery store. He later bought his own store in Delhi.

On December 27th, 1954 Russell married Thea Bolt. Thea died in July of 2000 and Russell followed soon after on November 19th 2000 in his 78th year.

CHRISTMAS Herbert William   Serv. # 127577

Givenchy-en-Gohelle Canadian Cemetery

Herbert was born on January 30th 1895 in Great Wigborough, Colchester England. He emigrated to Canada in 1913 to take up farming near the village of Washington and joined the Washington Methodist Church. On November 22nd 1915 Herbert enlisted as a private in the 71st Battalion at Woodstock, Ontario. His attestation papers showed him to have lungs that were healthy. He had the free use of his joints and limbs and he declared that he was not subject to fits of any description. He was 5 feet 11 inches tall with blue eyes and brown hair. His next of kin were Ellen and William Christmas of Great Wigborough in England. Herbert was killed in action in France on Thursday the 1st of March 1917 while serving with the 73rd Battalion Canadian Expeditionary Force (C.E.F.) as a Corporal. His name is inscribed on the cenotaph in Plattsville and also on a plaque in the Washington United Church. He is buried in Givenchy-en-Gohelle Canadian Cemetery, Souchez, Pas de Calais, France.

Washington Plaque

CHURCH Oscar Wilde   Serv. # 3106344

Chesterfield Cenotaph

Oscar was born on the 15th of July 1884 in Woodstock, Ontario. He was a painter by trade and moved to Bright. He enlisted at Hamilton, Ontario on the 5th of January 1918. Oscar was 5 feet 5 inches tall with a chest fully expanded of 38 1/2 inches. He was of dark complexion with blue eyes and brown hair. His mother was Jennie Burbanks, formerly Church, of 572 Hatch St. in Woodstock.

Oscar was killed in action on Wednesday the 28th of August 1918 while serving with the 20th Battalion of the Canadian Expeditionary Force (C.E.F.) as a private. His name is on the Cenotaph in Chesterfield and he is buried in the St. Olle British Cemetery in Raillencourt, France.

COLDHAM Donald Charles   Service No. V71152

Donald was born on September 19th 1921 on the family farm, just south of Washington, to Charles and Ruby Coldham. After finishing school he worked on the home farm for some time and then took courses in tool and die making. He then worked in Cambridge at his trade. Donald married Dorothy Gofton on November 23rd 1940. In early 1943 Donald joined the Royal Canadian Navy. He was a machinist and served on the Cataraqui, the Cornwallis, the Saguenay and the Scotian. The navy rated Donald as above average, a hard worker and reliable. Don received his honourable discharge on December 19th 1945. He then joined Firth and Brown Tools in Cambridge as a machinist.

He and his wife had a family of three children. The first, Charles Brian was born on August 21st 1943. Constance Marie arrived on April 22nd 1950. Betty Jean completed the family on September 5th 1953.

In due course Don was promoted to Superintendent of the plant at Firth and Brown. After many years he went into more advanced design and sales work in Toronto.

Donald died on November 22nd 1999.

COLDHAM John Walter   Serv. No. R155327

John was born on December 5th 1913 in Washington, Ontario to Charles and Ruby Coldham. After finishing school he worked for a time on the home farm. He moved to Tillsonburg and apprenticed as a mechanic at Stauffer Motors. He enlisted early in the war and trained in Aylmer on aero-engines. He was then posted to aero-engine school in Montreal as an instructor, a recognition of his competence. On July 12th 1943 John married Alice Boughner from Langton, Ontario. They lived in Montreal where he continued his duties as instructor. In June 1945 John was posted to Aylmer. Shortly thereafter he received his honourable discharge. John returned to Stauffer Motors in Tillsonburg as a mechanic.

On August 10th 1945 the first child, John Wayne, was born to John and Alice. After completing his education he took welding and lived in Glen Meyer. On November 29th 1948 Mary Lou was born. She took up nursing and now lives in Texas. Their third child, David Neil, was born on November 7th 1951 and now runs a very popular morning show on the Tillsonburg Radio Station.

John was promoted to Service Manager shortly after returning from the forces and retired from Stauffer Motors in the late seventies. He was sadly missed by the staff and customers.

John died on April 27th 1988 at 74 years of age.

CRAMPTON Frederick Serv.# 690038

Fred Crampton Killed 1917

Fred was born in Bright on March 23rd 1891. He was a printer by trade and married Laura Crampton. On February 3rd 1916 Fred joined the army at Drumbo. He was 5 feet 7 inches tall. His chest girth was 34 1/2 inches expanded with a 3 inch expansion. He had brown eyes, fair hair and a medium complexion.

This picture is hanging in the Bright United Church with pictures of the other members of the church killed in the First World War. Fred was killed in 1917.

A SHIFT OF WORKERS AT SHURLY-DIETRICH-ATKINS, IN CAMBRIDGE, JANUARY 1942 AROUND AN ARMOURED CAR THEY PRODUCED. DOUGLAS COXON IS IN THE PICTURE.

COXSON Douglas Edward

Douglas was born to Edward and Nellie on January 8th 1916 in Plattsville. His father, Edward, worked at the Plattsville Feed Mill and was a very good pitcher on the Plattsville Hard Ball team. Douglas used to work on the farm of his uncle Aubrey just north of Plattsville in the summers and after finishing school in 1932 he continued in agricultural work. At the beginning of the war he got a job with Shurly-Dietrich-Atkins Co. Ltd., a metal working plant in Cambridge. On February 22nd 1941 Douglas married Mary Ruth Doan. Their first son Gary Douglas was born on October 9th 1941.

In August 1942 Doug joined the Royal Canadian Air Force (R.C.A.F.) and was stationed at Brandon, Manitoba. He became ill and was honourably discharged for medical reasons in October the same year.

Douglas then rejoined Shurly-Dietrich-Atkins. On the facing page is a picture of the staff and a completed armoured car. Doug and Ruth had a second son, Bruce Edward on May 23rd 1945. Rick Leslie completed the family on February 6th 1952.

After the war Doug left Shurly-Dietrich-Atkins and went with Walker's Department store in the flooring division. In the early fifties he went with Galt Tile as a manager and retired from them in 1980.

Douglas died on October 19th 1995.

CRERAR John Stewart   Serv. # 797213

John was born in Perth County on January 23rd 1886. John had his B.A. and was a high school teacher in Port Rowan. He served in the 39th Regiment of the Militia until he enlisted in the 133rd Battalion of the Canadian Expeditionary Force (C.E.F.) at Simcoe on May 2nd 1916. He was 6 feet tall and a chest girth of 38 inches when fully expanded. His range of expansion was 4 inches. John had a fair complexion with blue eyes and brown hair. His next of kin were Jessie and Donald Crerar of Bright.

John was killed in action on the 9th of April 1917 at Vimy Ridge while serving in the 14th Battalion of the Canadian Expeditionary Force (C.E.F) as a private. He is buried in the Nine Elms Military Cemetery at Thelus Pas de Calais, France #523. His name is inscribed on the Cenotaph at Chesterfield and the Vimy Ridge Memorial.

The Canadian Memorial at Vimy Ridge covers 250 acres of land given by the French to Canada in perpetuity and has been planted with Canadian trees, one for each of the dead. The memorial was dedicated on July 26th 1936 by King Edward VIII.

Chesterfield Cenotaph

CUMMING Mary Doris

Doris was born on January 20th 1912. After finishing school she went into nursing and joined the Royal Canadian Army Medical Corps early in April 1942. As a nurse she was given the rank of Lieutenant, and called a Nursing Sister as was the custom in the British Army. She was stationed at the Military Hospital in Hamilton, Ontario.

Early in 1943 Doris was assigned to No. 2 Canadian General Hospital (C.G. H.), a 1,200 bed hospital which was being formed. It was comprised of Doctors, nurses and men from every province of Canada. The No. 2 C.G.H. was sent to England and took over the English Military Hospital in Bramshott near London. On D-Day the ambulances brought the wounded from the coast to Bramshott. Doris was all set to care for our boys but instead was assigned to a ward of German prisoners.

A couple of months later the No. 2 C.G.H. was sent to Normandy. They crossed the Channel on an English Hospital ship and landed on the shores of Normandy. They travelled to Bayeux in France where they set up the hospital in tents. Later in the fall the hospital was moved to Ghent in Belgium where they converted an Agricultural College into a hospital. They were not too far from the Battle of the Bulge. Shortly after Victory in Europe Day, Doris was transferred back to England to await transportation back to Canada. When she arrived in Ontario she was again assigned to the Military Hospital in Hamilton. Doris received her discharge in 1946.

The Bank of Nova Scotia

ESTABLISHED 1832

VANCOUVER, B.C.

August 22/46

Plattsville Community Committee,
Plattsville,
Ontario.

Dear friends:

I wish to thank you one
and all for the lovely Gruen watch which
I received in perfect condition. I am sorry
that it was not possible for me to be
there to receive it personally.

I am sure that the boys
from Plattsville who were in the service
have been treated more generously than
has been the custom in other Canadian
towns and cities, and we certainly appre-
ciate it. In future when anyone asks me
where I come from I shall throw out my
chest and say"I come from Plattsville,
the biggest little town in North America.

Yours very truly,

Geo Cumming

CUMMING George Cullen

George was born in October 1916. After completing school George got a job with the Bank of Nova Scotia in Kitchener in 1935. He joined the Canadian Army Pay Corps in 1941 with the rank of Staff Sergeant. He was stationed at the Military Hospital in Hamilton as pay master. He was sent to England in early 1943 and stationed at Aldershot in the Pay Corps. During his time in England George met and fell in love with a girl from London. He convinced her to come to Canada and wed him. He was posted back to Canada in late 1945 and immediately took his discharge. The Bank of Nova Scotia welcomed him back. In 1946 Sylvia Brookman came to Canada and married George in Kitchener.

CURRAH James Duncan

Jim was born on September 17th 1922 in Bright, Ontario to Roy and Leta Currah. He attended Continuation School in Bright (High School) and after finishing school he went to work at Whitelaw Machinery in Woodstock. In the spring of 1943 Jim joined the Royal Canadian Air Force (R.C.A.F.) and was posted to Manning Depot in Toronto. His next stop was Belleville for Initial Training School and after graduation he was posted to Ottawa for an electronics course. His next session of training took him to Mossbank, Saskatchewan for Bombing and Gunnery School after which he went to Winnipeg for navigation training. Having now graduated as a Bomb Aimer, Jim was sent to Three Rivers, Quebec to a holding unit to await transportation to England. In June 1944 he embarked on the New Amsterdam. A very crowded boat with troops sleeping on the decks under canvas.

On arrival in England he was sent to Bournemouth in Southern England. All Canadian Air Force personnel went to Bournemouth to await posting to more advanced training schools. Jim was posted to Rugby for O.T.U. (Operational Training Unit) flying Wellington two engined bombers. Here you were teamed up with a crew and trained with them for roughly two months. Wellingtons had been supplanted by the four engined bombers, the Halifax and Lancaster. Jim and his crew were posted to Conversion Unit at Tholthorpe in Yorkshire for training on the Halifax Mark 111. It had radial motors and was superior to the Mark 11 and Mark V that had Rolls Royce Merlins which were in-line. He and his crew were then sent to a holding unit. Shortly after this the war ended and he was posted to Bournemouth to await transportation home. In January 1946 he shipped home on the Queen Elizabeth, the largest ship afloat, and received his honourable discharge in February 1946.

Jim went back to Whitelaws for awhile as a machinist but decided to apprentice as a carpenter. He went into construction until 1952. This proved to be a good year for Jim. On June 27th 1952 he married Louise Theresa Parenteau. Their only child, Lynne Marie was born on April 26th 1954.

Jim, after leaving construction, went to work at the Post Office in 1952 and stayed with them until retirement in 1986. Louise died on May 13th 1996. In early 2004 Jim continues living at R.R.# 6, Woodstock.

CURRAH Willis John

James   **Willis**

Willis was born on October 2nd 1925 to Roy and Leta Currah in Bright, Ontario. After school he went to work with his older brother Jim at Whitelaw Machinery in Woodstock. Willis wanted to join up at 17, but he couldn't get his parents consent, so he lied about his age and joined in late 1942. He joined in London with the Oxford Rifles. In 1943 Willis was sent overseas and was transferred to the Governor Generals Foot Guards. They were a crack tank unit and were equipped with Sherman tanks. Shortly after D Day the unit was shipped to France and fought their way up through France, Belgium and Holland into Germany. He was shipped back home in the summer of 1945. Willis married Vivian Doreen Nichols on October 17th 1945. After his discharge in the beginning of 1946 he went back to Whitelaws Machinery for a spell. Willis and Vivian had five children. Terry Willis was born on May 24th 1946 and was tragically killed in an accident on October 5th 1981. Karen Gail was next and arrived on December 26th 1947. Karen died on December 23rd 1997, just shy of her 50th birthday. Grant Leroy then bowed in on December 14th 1948 followed by Leta Ruth Ann on July 16th 1950. Gary Jay completed the family on February 14th 1962.

After a few months at Whitelaws Willis took up farming. He rented land in the Burgessville and Mt. Elgin area and did cash cropping. He farmed until 1962 when he sold his equipment and started to work for United Co-op. He worked for them until his retirement in 1987. Vivian died in 1985. On February 3rd 1987 Willis married Clara Blanche Brooks.

He was awarded The 1939-45 Star, The France Germany Star, The Defence Medal, The Canadian Volunteer Service Medal with Clasp and the War Medal.

Willis died on December 9th 1992.

CUTHBERTSON Robert George Serv.# 447994

Robert Cuthbertson

Robert was born on February 26th 1890 to George W. and Mary Cuthbertson in Bright. He left home to work in Calgary about 1910. He enlisted in Calgary on the 9th of February 1916. Robert was 5 feet 9 1/2 inches tall, his chest when fully expanded was 37 inches in girth with an expansion of 4 inches.

He had a tattoo of a horses head on his right arm. Robert went overseas in August of 1916. He was killed in action on the Somme on Sunday the 19th of November 1916. His name is inscribed on the Vimy Ridge Memorial and on the Cenotaph in Victoria Park in Woodstock, Ontario. This picture is hanging in the Bright United Church alongside pictures of the other members of the church killed in the First World War.

Thomas Merton Cuthbertson

November 28, 1906 – March 21, 2000

"... a harvest of righteousness is sown in peace..."

JAMES 3:18

We remember Mert...

Thomas Merton (Mert) Cuthbertson enlisted in the Canadian Armed Forces on July 22, 1940 at the age of 34. His service number was B14165, and his service unit was the 5th Light Anti-Aircraft Regiment, 57th Division of the Royal Canadian Artillery. He saw service in World War 2 in Canada, England, Holland, Italy, France and Germany, and his decorations include 1939 - 1945 Star and Voluntary Service Medal; Italy, France and Germany Star and Defense Medal. He was discharged in November of 1945 with the rank of Bombadier.

He was Past Master of the Plattsville #178 Masonic Lodge, Past President of Branch 518 of the Royal Canadian Legion in Tavistock, Past Patron of the Order of the Easter Star in Innerkip, and was an active member of all three organizations.

After finally retiring, gardening became one of Mert's great passions. His family will all remember the good-natured arguments with brother Lorne about whose garden was the better, and Mert was often heard to boast about growing peas so big that he needed a pick-up truck just to carry each one. Mert was quick to pass along pieces of his gardening wisdom and advice, and just as quick to share the abundant produce he grew. In later years it was always amazing how any one who stopped just to talk with Mert in his garden, ended up helping him to hoe, pull weeds, tie up the tomatoes plants, or pick beets. Mert was working in his garden last June, when he fell and broke his hip. He had always enjoyed good health up to that point.

Until his late 80's, just to keep busy, Mert plowed snow in the winter and cut grass in the summers at North Blenheim Insurance, Bright United Church, and B&W Feeds. He was a very familiar figure, zipping around Bright on his lawn tractor. At one point, Mert was having a little problem getting his weed-eater started at North Blenheim, so a neighbour got it going for him, and watched in awe as Mert, after finishing his work, loaded the still running weed-eater in the back of his car. When questioned about the wisdom of putting a running power tool in the trunk of a car, Mert replied that he had to hurry to finish the lawn at the church, and didn't want to waste any more time fiddling with the darn machine. It was heard that Mert's lawn mower took a few unauthorized trips - without anyone at the controls.

Family meant everything to Mert. Throughout their 66 year marriage, Mert and Grace were close companions, especially during their retirement years. They shared an ongoing commitment to their children, grandchildren and great-grandchildren. Mert followed the lives of each member of the family with great interest and pride, as well as with a great sense of fun and humour. All the grandchildren and great-grandchildren remember Grandpa Cub's horsebites, which he had perfected over his 93 years (and, while demonstrations tend to be painful, feel free to ask any family member about his technique).

At this time, surrounded by friends and family, we have come to have a new appreciation of the fun-loving, humorous, and truly special person that Mert Cuthbertson was. While overwhelmed by the space Mert's passing leaves in our family, we celebrate the wonderful life he lived and are truly thankful to have been a part of it. Mert will forever live on in our hearts and continue to inspire us as we go on.

Memorial Service for Thomas Merton Cuthbertson
2:00 p.m., Saturday, March 25, 2000

Organ Prelude
Scripture Sentences
Words of Greeting
Opening Prayer (unison)

Eternal God, we give you thanks for the gift of life, and acknowledge the uncertainties of life on earth. Most of all, O God, we thank you that beyond this life, there is new life with you, as you receive us in your mercy and love. May your presence be felt among us this day as we gather in sorrow, celebration and thanksgiving. Amen.

Hymn: *In the Garden*
Reflections of the Family
Scripture Readings:

Lamentations 3: 21-26
Psalm 71 (selected verses)

In you, O Lord, I take refuge
Let me never be put to shame.
In your righteousness, deliver me.
Incline your ear to me and save me.
Be to me a rock of refuge, a strong fortress to save me.
For you are my rock and my fortress.
You, O Lord, are my hope, my trust, O Lord, from my youth.
Upon you I have leaned from my birth. My praise is continually of you.
O God, from my youth you have taught me.
And I still proclaim your wondrous deeds.
So even to old age and gray hairs, O God, do not forsake me.
Until I proclaim your might to all the generations to come.

John 14 (selected verses)

Meditation
Prayers of Thanksgiving and Intercession *The Lord's Prayer*
Hymn: *Make Me a Channel of Your Peace*
Benediction

Participants:

Minister	Joan Berge
Organist	Connie Vollmershausen
Pallbearers	*The Grandchildren:*

Randy Simpson	Tracy Fulton Porteous	Todd Fulton
Scott Simpson	Brendan Pennylegion	Lee Fulton

You are invited to join the family for a time of food and fellowship in the church basement following the service of committal at the Chesterfield Cemetery.

Thomas Merton (Mert) Cuthbertson died peacefully, on Tuesday, March 21, 2000, at St. Mary's General Hospital, Kitchener. He resided at 8 George Street, Bright.

Mert was born on a farm just outside of Hickson 93 years ago, a son of the late Tom and Ida Cuthbertson. Other than a few years in North Dakota, and 5 years in the Canadian Armed Forces, Mert spent his life in Bright and surrounding area. He worked as a farm hand, at the cheese factory and retired from the job of Postmaster of the Bright Post Office. Not one to sit still, Mert then took on the job of mail carrier for several more years. He took great pride and pleasure in his garden and often shared the produce of his labour with family and friends. He was a member of the United Church, Bright.

Beloved husband of Grace (Klosz) with whom he celebrated 66 years of marriage (March 15, 1934). Loving father of Connie and Bill Simpson of Washington, Gail Fulton of Bright and Gwen and Sean Pennylegion of Woodview. "Grandpa Cub" will be missed by grandchildren Randy and Julie Simpson, and Scott Simpson, all of Plattsville, and by Lee Fulton, Todd Fulton, and Joel Howard, all of London, Tracy and Cameron Porteous of Queenston, and Brendan Pennylegion of Toronto. "Great-Grandpa Cub" will be dearly missed by great-grandsons David Buck and Tim Simpson of Plattsville, and Harrison Porteous of Queenston. Also missed by sisters-in-law, Margaret Richardson of Ottawa, and Belle Cuthbertson of London.

Mert was predeceased by brothers and sisters Evans, Edna, Muriel, Lorne, Jack, and Merle; father-in-law and mother-in-law William and Anne Klosz, sister-in-law Blanche Cuthbertson, brothers-in-law Ray Johnson and Harold Weiss, and son-in-law LaVerne Fulton.

Thank You

We extend our sincere thanks for the prayers and support of family and friends during Mert's stay in hospital and since his death. You have shown your love and kindness in many ways and we will always remember.

Grace Cuthbertson and family

CUTHBERTSON Thomas Merton Service # B15165

Mert was born in Hickson on November 28th 1906. He went to school in Windfall, Bright and high school in Drumbo. On March 15th 1934 he married Ethel Grace Wilma Isabelle Klosz. This was in the depths of the depression. To make a living he took any work he could get. Mert whitewashed barns as this was the time when milking parlours became popular and there was much to be done. He also worked on farms threshing in the fall. Mert and Grace had three daughters, Constance Virginia born September 27th 1936, Margaret Gail came on November 7th 1938 and after the war Gwen Elizabeth was born on March 23rd 1948.

On July 22nd, 1940 Mert joined the Canadian Army. He served with the 5th Light Anti-Aircraft Regiment, 57th Division of the Royal Canadian Artillery. He went overseas in September 1941 and saw service in England, Italy, Holland and Germany. In England Mert was first stationed at Biggin Hill, then various training stations. As he was a very competent motorcyclist he was utilized as an instructor training soldiers who were required to use them. He came home in September 1945 and was discharged in November of that year with the rank of Corporal.

The family settled in Bright and Mert drove truck for a living. He also did custom work for Roy Facey. In the spring of 1946 Mert bought a farm under the Veteran's Land Act. In November of 1945 he got a mail route. Of course Grace helped on the route. In 1954 Mert took over as Post Master in Bright. He still kept the mail route. He was Post master for 17 years then had to retire at 65 year of age. He kept the mail route and ran it until he was 78 years young. Mert was very active in the Plattsville Legion and when it was disbanded he joined the Tavistock Legion.

Merton died on March 21st 2000 in his 94th year.

DAVIDSON Henry (Harry) Lee

Harry was born May 2nd 1918. After finishing school he went to work at Canada Sand. In December of 1942 Harry enlisted in the Royal Canadian Air Force (R.C.A.F.) and after suitable training became a transport driver and was posted overseas in December 1943 as a Leading Aircraftsman. He was attached to the second tactical air force which provided cover for the Canadian army in France. The tactical squadrons were usually equipped with Mustang or Typhoon fighters and were used to destroy enemy armoured units. They followed the army into Belgium, Holland and Germany. Harry Lee returned home in March 1946 and received his discharge. He then went back to work at Canada Sand as a lead hand and in due course was promoted to foreman.

Harry married Elva Margaret Roth in 1938. They had a perfectly balanced family of five girls and five boys. Kenneth McAlister started off the parade on February 9th 1939. Gerald Roth followed on April 13th 1940. Harold Lee was next and arrived on August 19th 1941. Donna Maxine, the first girl, was born on May 31st 1944 followed by a sister Cheryl Marlene on March 3rd 1947. Janice Dalene then showed up on January 20th 1949. Bruce Wayne was next on April 14th 1951. Wanda Dawn was born on September 6th 1956 and Charleen Lynn was the last of the girls on February 26th 1958. Brent Marlin completed the family on August 24th 1963.

Harry Lee was a fiddle player and enjoyed country and western music. He joined a group of musicians in the area and became their band leader shortly after. They played at many dances. He retired from Canada Sand in 1983.

Harry Lee died on August 31st 1999.

DAVIS Vernon John Serv.# 2500576

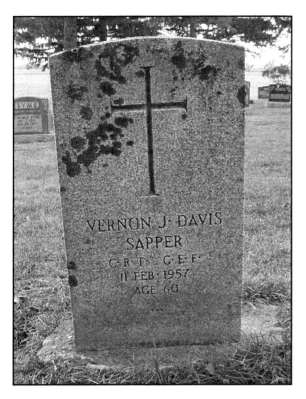

Vernon was born in Sweaburg, Ontario on May 9th 1896. His mother later became Mrs. Ida Edwards. After completing his education he became a hired hand on local farms. He enlisted in the army in January 1916 and became a Sapper in the Canadian Expeditionary Force (C.E.F.). When he enlisted he was 5 feet 6 in. tall. The girth of his chest when fully expanded was 35 1/2 inches with a range of expansion of 2 1/2 inches. Vernon had a fair complexion with blue eyes and brown hair. After his honourable discharge in 1919 he went back to agricultural work as a hired man in the Plattsville area. He remained a hired man all his life.

Vernon died on February 11th 1957 at 60 years of age. His funeral was ordered and paid for by the Royal Canadian Legion. They also bought a headstone and burial plot in the Chesterfield Cemetery.

DEWAR Arnott Comrie Serv.# 127346

Plattsville Memorial Gates

Arnott was born on September 14th 1893 in Chippewa, Ontario to Dr. and Mrs. M.C. Dewar of Bright. After finishing school he joined the Canadian Bank of Commerce. On October 15th 1915, at 22 years of age, Arnott joined the 71st Battalion of the Canadian Expeditionary Force. He was 5 feet 5 1/2 inches tall with a girth when fully expanded of 35 1/2 inches with a range of expansion of 4 1/2 inches. Arnott was of fair complexion with blue eyes and light brown hair. Arnott was a Presbyterian.

DEWAR Robert Archibald Serv.# 772135

Plattsville Memorial Gates

Robert was born on April 8th 1891 in Pickering, Ontario to Mr. and Mrs. D.M. Dewar of Bright, Ontario. After finishing school Bob became a cheese maker. He joined the army in Brantford on October 20th 1915. Bob was 5 feet 5 inches tall, the girth of his chest when fully expanded was 38 inches with a range of expansion of 4 1/4 inches. He had a fair complexion with grey eyes and light hair. Bob was a Presbyterian.

DOBSON Henry

Henry was born on June 3rd 1923 in Toronto. On July 1st 1929 the family moved to Wolverton. In March 1943 Henry joined the Royal Canadian Air Force (R.C.A.F.) and was sent to Manning Depot in Toronto. His group were given Link training at the Normal School. That gave the Air Force an indication of your suitability to be a pilot.

He was then posted to Victoriaville, Quebec for Initial Training School from which he graduated in December 1943. The next posting was to Elementary Flying Training School at Regina graduating in May 1944. He was posted to Gimli, Manitoba for six weeks and then to Alleford Bay in the Queen Charlotte Islands. Henry was, and still is, deeply moved by the spectacular beauty of these Islands. He flew in Canso and Catalina flying boats patrolling the Pacific Ocean off the Canadian coast. He was a gunner and kept a lookout for Japanese submarines and paper balloons with bombs attached to them that the Japanese launched to terrorize the people of the Canadian West. They hoped to make a few lucky hits on populated areas or start forest fires.

In October 1944 Henry was posted to Service Flying Training School in Claresholm, Alberta, graduating in March 1945. He volunteered for Pacific duty, but V.J. day finished the need for that and Henry was honourably discharged in September 1945. Henry loved the rural countryside and wanted to live there, so he went back to Wolverton and bought a farm of 150 acres through the Veterans Land Act on the blind 9th Concession. He decided raising turkeys would provide a good living. This was a very successful operation. Unfortunately, after a few years, his flock was hit with a disease that put him out of the turkey business. Henry had always had an interest in antiques and in 1957 started a business from the farm. In 1959 he married Martini Geradina Vandergeest. They had two daughters, Monique Anne, born on November 16th 1960 and Mignon Camille born on May 23rd 1962. His wife died in December 1963. Henry then bought the old hotel in Plattsville and opened his antique store in November 1964. He became one of the most respected and successful antique dealers in Ontario. On November 6th 1965 Henry married Barbara Anne Kerr. On February 7th, 1967 they had a son Dane Courtney. In 1998 Henry and Barbara sold the building in Plattsville and moved to their 25 acre farm on Gibson Lane just a few miles east of Drumbo. Henry has returned to his "roots" - living in the country beside the Nith River, just as he had done in Wolverton.

DUNN Lawrence Sidney Serv.# R-118609

Larry was born on January 17th 1918 to Austin and Nellie Dunn from Linwood. After finishing school he worked at Canada Sand. He joined the Royal Canadian Air Force on July 14th 1941 and on August 31st 1941 he married Marion Irene Patterson from Plattsville. He was a Leading Aircraftsman in the Royal Canadian Air Force (R.C.A.F). for four years and three months, spending a few months in England. He volunteered for the Pacific but with Victory in Japan (V.J.) Day intervening he was given his discharge on February 19th 1946.

Larry and Marion had four children. Shirley Elizabeth was born on February 14th 1943. Suzanne Nell came on October 20th 1950. Arthur William, the first son, was born on May 6th 1953 and James Gordon completed the family on May 23rd 1957.

Larry obtained a farm through the Veterans Land Act (V.L.A.) at Monticello. He farmed till 1959 then sold the farm and moved to Fergus where he worked for the Grand River Conservation Authority until the late 1960's when he went into construction as Martin Dunn Construction. Shortly after he left construction and was hired by the Wellington County Board of Education as a custodian. He retired from the board in 1983. Marion, his wife of fifty years died on September 27th 1991. Larry later moved to the Wellington Terrace in Elora.

Larry died on February 26th 2004.

EDWARDS George Ward

George was born on June 16th 1905 in Plattsville. On January 17th 1928 he married Mary Ida Duncan and they had two children. A daughter, Donna Blanche, was born on December 23rd 1928, a son, Floyd Ward was born on September 26th 1931. George worked at Canada Sand in 1936 earning seventeen cents an hour. He joined the Oxford Rifles in March 1942 and was sent on a commando course in Listowel, where he was promoted to Sergeant. He was next sent to London, Prince George and Long Branch on courses. Then it was back to Prince George, on to Wainwright, Courtney and Nanaimo, where he was hospitalized before being sent home and honourably discharged.

George went back to work at Canada Sand. His outdoor activities included hunting, curling and lawn bowling. He also enjoyed a good game of bridge.

George died on January 17th 1965.

ELLIS Roy Charles   Serv.# 675655

Roy was born on June 4th 1896 on the home farm, Lot 21 Concession 9 East Zorra Township, to Jonathan and Sarah Jane Ellis. On February 28th 1916, Roy joined the 168th Battalion known as "Oxford's Own". Roy was 5 feet 5 inches tall and his chest girth was 38 inches when fully expanded with a 4 inch range of expansion. He had a fair complexion, blue eyes and blond hair. On June 1st 1916, the Battalion started a brief training at Camp Francis near London, Ontario. They were then moved to Camp Borden for four months of intensive training. The 168th embarked aboard the S.S Lapland on October 30th 1916 from Halifax, Nova Scotia bound for Liverpool, England.

On arrival, the 168th was absorbed by the 12th and 39th Reserve Battalions. Roy was transferred to the 39th. They completed their training at West Sanding Camp, England. Crossing the channel to France, Roy was transferred to the 2nd Canadian Battalion Eastern Ontario Regiment, Canadian Expeditionary Force. In the battle for Vimy Ridge on April 28th the 1st and 2nd Battalions, on the left flank, attacked Arleux-en-Gobelle, beyond Willerval. The Canadians captured the town and a large number of German troops. There was further furious fighting in the area and on May 3rd 1917 Roy was killed. Roy has no known grave. His name is inscribed on the Vimy Ridge Memorial and the Cenotaph in Chesterfield and Plattsville. He was a member of the Washington Church and his name is inscribed on a plaque in the church.

Washington Plaque

ELLIS Thomas Roy

Tom was born on February 18th 1918 to Oliver and Jessie Violet Ellis. He joined the Royal Canadian Regiment in June 1940 and spent one year training at Camp Borden in the Three Rivers Tank Corps. He was then posted to England and assigned to the 12th Armoured Regiment. In August 1942 he was shipped to Sicily and then on to Italy in 1943. The Italian fighting was brutal as the mountainous terrain heavily favoured the defense. Armoured units were at a distinct disadvantage as they had no room to manoeuvre.

After fighting all the way up the Italian Peninsula the Canadian troops were shipped to Marsailles and went through France to Belgium and Holland to engage the enemy. Tom was shipped home and received his honourable discharge on September 11th 1945.

He was hired by Erb's Garage in Waterloo as a motor mechanic. On August 23rd 1952 Tom wed Catherine Elizabeth Schneider. They had no children.

Tom died in the Veterans Hospital in London, Ontario on January 16th 1982.

ENGLISH John Henry (Jack) Serv.# 82005

Jack was born on April 14th 1916 to John Bain and Clara Catherine English. After finishing school Jack worked in his father's general store in Plattsville.

On August 10th 1940 Jack married Vivian Merle Kennedy. He joined the Oxford Rifles and was posted to Listowel on a Commando Course. He was promoted to Sergeant and spent the next three months in Wolsey Barracks in London. He was then posted to Prince George, British Columbia for a further year of training. After this he spent 6 months in Nanaimo, then to Courtney and back to Prince George where he became a Quartermaster Sergeant. Jack went overseas in December 1944 to #9 Infantry Training Battalion at Petworth in England and was promoted to Regimental Quartermaster. Shortly after his arrival he got word that his first son John had been born on January 26th 1945.

Jack was sent home in April 1946 and was given an honourable discharge. He then went into partnership with his father John B. English in Plattsville in the grocery and general store. On October 21st 1948 a second son, Robert was born to Merle and Jack. Jack's father had taken over the store in 1914 and Jack ran it till 1975 when he sold it to pursue a life of leisure. He was very active in town affairs and was elected to the Township Council where he served for a few years. He was also Secretary of the Hockey League that played in the Plattsville Arena for many years. At 85 Jack was a very good and active curler, still being skip of his own rink.

The eldest son, John, got his Ph.D. in History and is a professor at the University of Waterloo. He served as an M.P. for five years. He has written several historical books, one a biography of Lester B. Pearson and one on William Lyon Mackenzie King. He is also Chairman of the Museum of Civilization in Hull, Quebec. The younger son Robert is an M.D. in Fergus.

Merle passed away on August 20th 2003 with Jack by her side.

EVERTS Albert Milton

Allie was born on March 24th 1912 at Rainham Centre, Haldimand County, Ontario. After school he worked at the Dominion Linseed Oil Co. in Baden. He was very inventive and made knives from saw blades that are still used in the family.

Allie married Margaret Fenn of Plattsville on December 19th 1941. Allie joined the Royal Hamilton Light Infantry in July 1942. He was stationed at Niagara-on-the-Lake initially, then on to Debert, Mulgrave and Sydney in Nova Scotia. While at Debert he received word that his son Keith was born on November 6th 1942. He went overseas in May 1943 and was stationed at Aldershot and Whitley in England for training. On June 6th 1944 the unit landed at Juno Beach. Allie fought from Caen to Falaise through some of the heaviest fighting of the war, then on into Belgium and Holland. While taking shelter from heavy fire in the basement of a house in Holland a mortar shell came through a window, killing all but Allie. When dug out on October 19th 1944 he was in extremely serious condition. Private Everts was unable to see and had severe head, arm, leg and hip injuries and was badly burned.

He was given blood plasma and flown to Antwerp, then to Croyden, England to the burn unit at Basingstoke Hospital. He owes his life to penicillin having received this drug every 3 hours for 40 consecutive days. He was sent home as a stretcher case on board the Hospital Ship, Llandovery Castle on January 11th 1945. He was taken to Chorley Park Military Hospital where he underwent 8 eye operations and 14 operations on his face, arms, and legs including bone grafts on one arm. He was also given a new nose.

When Allie was well enough he took the position of Postmaster in the Village of Baden and was there until he retired.

Anne was born on May 27th 1947, another daughter Jane was born on June 13th 1951. The twins, Nancy and Neil, arrived on January 5th 1953.

Allie died December 21st 1960, Margaret on January 29th 1996.

Medals awarded were the Canadian Volunteer Service Medal (CVSM) and Clasp, France-Germany Star, 1939-45 Star and the War Medal 1939-45.

FAIR Frederick Alexander

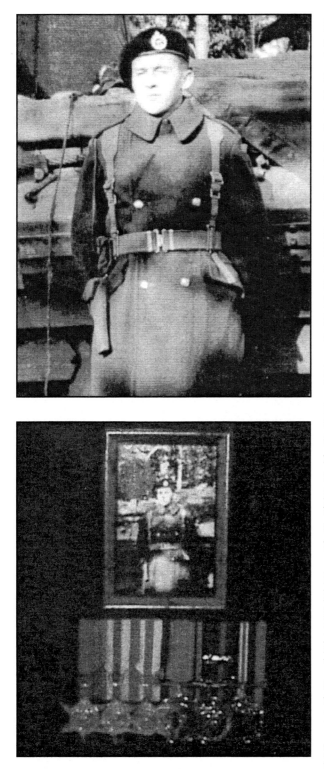

Sandy was born on July 3rd 1922. He joined the army at 17 years of age in the Dental Corps. When he reached 18 he transferred to an Ontario unit called the Black Cats. They were a tank regiment with American Sherman tanks. He went overseas with them and they fought their way through Sicily and Italy. Italy was not tank country so they were tested to the utmost. When the Italian campaign was successfully completed they were shipped to Marsailles, France and went through France to Belgium and fought their way to Nijmegen where the war ended. Sandy (Fred) came home on the Louis Pasteur in September 1945 and received his honourable discharge on the 10th of October. Sandy was awarded the 1939-1945 Star, the Italy Star, the France, Germany Star, The Canadian Volunteer Service Medal and Clasp, the Defense Medal and the War Medal 1939-45.

He then bought a farm near Guelph under the Veterans Land Act. He ran a dairy farm raising pure bred Holsteins. In 1953 Sandy sold the Guelph farm and bought a farm on the 13th Concession just east of Chesterfield. He remained in dairy farming until 1957 when he sold his herd and switched to hogs. It was a good change, so Sandy bought the Bell farm on the 12th Concession. He had 80 to 100 brood sows on the home farm and shipped the wieners to the Bell farm for fattening.

In 1948 Sandy married Olive Edith Weicker. On May 20th 1949 they had a daughter Rose Lynn. She was followed by Robin Alexander on April 11th 1950, then Alan James came along on February 11th 1953, with another son Patrick Willis born on May 10th 1956. Lisa Jane, the second girl, came on December 6th 1958 with two boys following, John William on April 10th 1963 and Ian Robert on November 4th 1965.

In 1969 Sandy and Olive went to Italy and England. Olive said they slept in 20 different beds in 21 days. They covered the route Sandy took with the Black Cat regiment fighting up the Italian peninsula. They landed at Pizza and rented a car which was stolen in Rome. They went on to Milan and then flew to England from Florence. Olive said it was a wonderful trip that they enjoyed immensely.

Sandy died in November 1990.

FENN Edward Gillis Serv.# A106423

Ed was born on September 24th 1925 at Plattsville to Gillis and Etta Fenn. He was quite active in sports and particularly enjoyed baseball and hockey. As the family had owned the butcher business for upwards of eighty years it was natural for Ed to work in the family business prior to enlisting.

Ed enlisted at London, Ontario on March 24th 1943. As a Private in the Army, Edward was sent to Chatham, Ontario for basic training and then posted to Ipperwash for advanced training. Because he was underage for overseas duty he was sent to Debert, Canso, Mulgrave and Sydney, Nova Scotia for varied duties. For instance at Canso the duty was to check the coastline for landings from U-Boats. He was then transferred to Camp Borden, was trained and certified as a Driver, wheeled vehicles, including motorcycle operator and further qualified as a Signalman. In September 1944 he went to England on the Mauretania, landing at Liverpool. In October he sailed from Scotland in a convoy to Italy, landing at Naples. He joined the signal platoon of the Perth Regiment at the Lamone River. Ed contracted tuberculosis in Italy.

In February the Perths moved to Leghorn and sailed on an LST (Landing Ship Tank) to Marseilles, France. The Regiment went in truck convoy to Kemmel in Belgium, regrouped, and fought up through Holland to Delfzijl on the German border. On April 28th 1945 Ed was wounded at Nansum. He was fortunate that he had a radio on his back for protection against the shrapnel that got him in the legs and knees.

Ed was repatriated in September 1945 and honourably discharged on November 15th 1945. Medals awarded to Ed were the Canadian Volunteer Service Medal and Clasp, Italy Star, France Germany Star and the War Medal 1939-45. On November 17th 1945 he married Laura Rennick of Bright. They had two sons, David Edward was born on March 27th 1948 and Donald John was born on September 10th 1949. Ed worked at the family butcher business and took it over in 1951. In 1952 Ed had a reoccurrence of his tuberculosis and was hospitalized until 1955. In 1953 he had to sell the business that had been in the family for over 80 years. In 1957 Ed started with Canada Agriculture as a fruit and vegetable inspector. He retired in 1980. Laura passed away on May 14th 1998. Ed moved to North Bay where his two sons live. In 2003 he is enjoying life with them.

FENN Graham Serv.# A-82021

Graham was born on January 25th 1920 in Plattsville to Gillis and Etta Fenn. Being the eldest of three sons he naturally worked in the family butcher shop in Plattsville. He was a member of the Oxford Rifles Reserve for twenty months prior to his enlistment in Woodstock on April 6th 1942. He was posted to London and then Prince George, British Columbia where his unit was to make preparations to establish a post in the Aleutian Islands. While in British Columbia he took a course on Bren Gun Carriers. In May the Government abandoned the project on the Aleutians so Graham and others were sent home on embarkation leave and posted to England. Graham's younger brother Ed was stationed in England at the same time. When on leave together they visited other service men from Plattsville. Shortly after, their brother-in-law Allie Everts, was sent back to England with very serious injuries. They were vitally concerned for Allie and his wife Margaret, who was their sister back in Canada.

Letters were so important to our parents at home. If there was no mail they worried, if there was mail they were fearful of bad news. It was a stressful time for them. Graham's mother kept the last letter Graham wrote while he was still in the army as he was the last member of the family to come home. The letter is still treasured. Graham came back from overseas in February 1946. He received his honourable discharge shortly after.

In later years Graham told the story of his return from active service. When the train stopped in Galt (now Cambridge) he got off to phone home. Jessie McMeekin, the telephone operator at Plattsville, recognized his voice and interrupted his call when she realized where he was and said, " Get back on the train, Graham, your parents and brother Ed and Laura are on their way to London to meet you". Graham dropped the receiver and ran out of the station. He caught the last car as the train pulled away. His family was indeed waiting for him at the station in London.

Graham got back into the butcher business. He opened a shop in London and then one in St. Thomas. On December 27th 1947 Graham married Alma Jean Jones. Their first child, Janet, was born on October 28th 1948. James followed on July 3rd 1950. Ruth joined the clan on March 15th 1952 and Robert made his debut on July 28th 1953. Mary Margaret completed the family on February 28th 1959. Graham sold London and St. Thomas and opened a shop in Hamilton and then Burlington.

Graham died on August 12th 1996.

FENN James Hugh   Service # V17696

James was born on October 14th 1922 in Plattsville to Gillis and Etta Fenn.   After school Jim liked to hunt and fish and play tricks on other people. Prior to enlisting he worked in Kitchener at Dumarts Meat Packing. Jim joined the navy as a stoker in May of 1941. He was sent to Halifax and served on H.M.C.S. Stadacona then H.M.C.S. Venture. He was transferred to H.M.C.S Restigouche, a destroyer well known for its fighting capabilities. Jim served on it from October 1941 until May 1943. This was the only ship he served on in the battle of the Atlantic, the Murmansk Run to Northern Russia and the Mediterranean Theatre. When engaged with the enemy his position was with the Depth Charge detail. Of course the Murmansk run was murder. Losses were 90% of the freighters on every run. He sailed to Ireland, Africa and the Mediterranean. He was on the Iceland Patrol for four months and the Clyde Patrol for three months. James was promoted to a Bi-rating. He did Convoy Duty in the Atlantic Ocean, the Bay of Biscay and the Mediterranean. During one particularly violent storm Jim was washed overboard but very fortuitously was washed right back on deck by a very timely wave. His ship was once badly damaged in battle and refitted in Ireland.

While in the Mediterranean area Jim became ill and was diagnosed as having tuberculosis. He was flown back to England and was in hospitals in England and Scotland. He came home in 1944 aboard the Hospital Ship, the Lady Nelson. Jim spent the best part of two years in Freeport Sanatorium in Kitchener, and was finally discharged to resume civilian life.

Jim was awarded the Canadian Volunteer Service Medal (CVSM) and Clasp, the War Medal 1939-45, the Africa Star, the Atlantic Star, the 1939-45 Star, and the Russians awarded him the Murmansk Medallion.

Jim married Reta Daniells of New Hamburg on August 4th 1945. On March 29th 1946 Patricia Margaret was born. Richard James followed on September 26th 1947 and a second son, Mark Edward, completed the family on June 25th 1954.

Jim formed a Construction Company at Plattsville and Waterford in the 1950's and worked at it until retirement.

Reta died in June 1975 and Jim, in his 70th year, on December 19th 1991.

FENN John Howard

John was born on September 18th 1917 in Plattsville. After obtaining his Grade 13 at Plattsville Continuation School he went on to Western in London and took six courses. He then attended Normal School in Stratford and after successful completion taught school for four and a half years. In 1937 he taught at S.S. No. 8 in Waterloo County. He then moved to Douglas School in Fort Erie from 1938 to 1940 where he was Assistant Principal.

On September 6th 1941 he enlisted in the Royal Canadian Air Force (R.C.A.F.) at the Hamilton Recruiting Centre. He went to Manning Depot in Toronto and was selected to be trained as a radar mechanic. He trained for four months at the University of Toronto as this was a very new technology and the U. of T. had competent people in this area. He was then stationed at Clinton. In March of 1942 he was posted overseas and sent to Bournemouth on the South coast of England as were all Air Force personnel. In May of 1942 he was posted to the radar station in Hibaldstow. The Germans became aware of this radar station in Northern England and bombed it. After one year with the Royal Air Force (R.A.F.) John received his commission as a Pilot Officer and was transferred to 406 Squadron, a Canadian Squadron of fighter command. He served with 406 Squadron until the close of the war. He returned to Canada in August 1945 and was discharged with the rank of Flight Lieutenant in October. He received the 1939-45 Star, the Canadian Volunteer Service Medal and Clasp and the War Medal 1939-45.

In November of 1945 John returned to his position at the Douglas School in Fort Erie. In 1946 he accepted a position as a Service Bureau Officer with the Ontario Command of the Canadian Legion and became the Secretary of the Service Bureau Committee.

John married Edith Ruth Craig on June 28th 1947 in Dundas. Their only child, Marilyn Ruth, was born on December 31st 1950. On April 1st 1949 John accepted a job with the National Research Council Atomic Energy project in Chalk River and remained there until his retirement in 1982.

John died on October 27th 1989. His wife, Edith, died on February 9th 1995.

FERGUSSON James Blair

Blair was born on November 23rd 1919 at home on Lot 21, Concession 13 of Blenheim Township, 1 mile from Plattsville to James Edward and Jean (nee-Decker) Fergusson. After completing school Blair worked in retail hardware until he joined the Royal Canadian Air Force on November 8th 1942. He was posted to Brandon Manning Depot. He took his wireless course in Winnipeg and completed it on October 26th 1943. He was then posted to Paulson, Manitoba for Bombing and Gunnery School. He graduated from B. and G. School on December 13th 1943 and received his Wireless Air Gunner (WAG) Wing and was promoted to Sergeant. He was then posted to Ancienne Lorette in Quebec and was on staff until January 17th 1944. From there he went to Air Navigation School at Malton. In October 1944 Blair was posted overseas and took his A.F.U at Bishop's Court. Upon completion he went to Long Marston for Operational Training on Wellington Bombers. His last flight was June 1945. By this time Blair had been promoted to Warrant Officer. He came home on the Ile de France in October 1945 and received his honourable discharge on November 8th 1945.

He went into the Hardware business with Cochrane Dunlop Hardware Ltd. On September 4th 1946 Blair married Jessie Elizabeth Talbot from Leaside. Shortly after they were sent to Sudbury with C.D.H. Ltd. On September 22nd 1948 Jane Elizabeth was born. Howard James followed on January 12th 1952 and Mary Louise completed the family on May 2nd 1954. In 1975 Blair left Cochrane Dunlop and went into real estate. After a successful career in real estate Blair retired in October of 1984. As of 2003 Blair and Jessie reside in Markham.

FERGUSSON Edwin James

Edwin was born on November 25th 1913 to William and Susan (nee-Hunt) Fergusson in Blenheim Township. Ed loved music and became an accomplished pianist and trumpet player. After finishing High School he went to the Toronto Conservatory of Music and took advanced courses in piano, vocal, brass and organ for six years. He was also giving piano lessons and teaching music in the public schools at this time. In 1937 Ed was appointed Supervisor of Music in Elementary schools in Waterloo County. On August 25th 1937 Ed married Anne Mary MacFarlane. In 1939 he joined the Oxford Rifles, a militia unit in Plattsville. He became a 2nd Lieutenant in the reserves. He joined the regular army on April 6th 1942 and retained his rank of 2nd Lieutenant from the militia. He was posted to London, Prince George and Gordon Head, where he was promoted to First Lieutenant. His next posting was to Camp Borden then overseas in January 1943. He landed in France on 'D' Day and was promoted to Captain. Edwin served in France and Belgium. After Victory in Europe (VE) Day he volunteered for Pacific duty. He arrived home on July 26th 1945 for a 30 day leave, before training for the Pacific. Japan collapsed so Ed received his honourable discharge in September 1945.

On February 18th 1946 George William was born. Margaret Anne followed on November 6th 1948 and the family was completed when James Robert was born on August 2nd 1952. By this time Ed was teaching in Secondary Schools and playing lead trumpet in a band. He taught for the Department of Education from 1954 to 1959 in Summer School. He also taught summer school at Mount Allison University in Sackville, New Brunswick from 1960 to 1966. He got heavily involved in the Royal Canadian Legion, the Masonic Lodge and the Eastern Star. He was a past master of the Plattsville Lodge, a life member and organist of Wilmot Lodge #318. He was a member and director of the Baden Chamber of Commerce and was the past patron and organist of the Nith Valley Chapter of the order of the Eastern Star. Ed received the Bi-Centennial Medal in 1984. He retired from teaching in 1978, but kept giving private lessons.

Ed died on November 7th 1987 in his 74th year.

FERGUSSON Frederick Newton

Fred was born on June 22nd 1910 to William and Susan Fergusson. After completing University and Teachers College he obtained a job teaching in West Montrose in 1935. He also married Elizabeth Julia Bulgen on August 14th 1935. The contract with the West Montrose school stipulated a salary of $800.00 a year and Fred also had to assume the duties of the superintendent of the United Church Sunday School. Their first child, Donald Richard was born on June 3rd 1936. John Douglas, who was born on March 18th 1940, was adopted shortly after birth.

Fred joined the army in 1941 and was given his commission as 2nd Lieutenant at Brockville. After posting to Camp Borden Fred was promoted to 1st Lieutenant. He was posted to Terrace, British Columbia and then Woodstock for further training. He was sent to the Royal Military College at Kingston where he served as Intelligence Officer. Posted overseas in July 1943 Fred landed in France on D Day with the Artillery. He served in Belgium, Holland and Germany where he was promoted to Captain. He volunteered for Pacific duty and arrived home on July 26th 1945 for thirty days leave before training for the Pacific. As Victory in Japan (V.J.) Day intervened Fred was sent to London, England to write the official history of the Canadian Army in Europe with Colonel Stacey. He returned home in 1947 and received his honourable discharge.

Fred then was hired to teach at Forest Hill Public School in Toronto. He and Elizabeth adopted two more children, Marilyn Elizabeth born on June 8th 1951 and Caroline Diane born on March 12th 1952. In due course Fred took a teaching position at Scarborough and was promoted to Principal.

Fred died on August 4th 1981.

FERGUSSON Russell William Serv.# A-82271

Russell was born on July 27th 1916 to William and Susan Fergusson. He joined the Royal Canadian Air Force (R.C.A.F.) in May of 1941. After initial training Russ was promoted to Corporal and stationed at Rockliffe. His brothers convinced him he would have better opportunities in the army so in June 1942 he transferred to the Oxford Rifles. In both services he served a total of four years and nine months. When Russ transferred to the Army he lost his rank and went down to private. On March 24th 1942 he was promoted to Corporal and was posted to Prince George, British Columbia. He was promoted to Acting Sergeant on March 24th 1943 and on August 1st 1943 Russ was made a full Sergeant. Later he was stationed in London and after Victory in Europe Russ volunteered for the Pacific. He received his honourable discharge on October 17th 1945.

On March 2nd 1940 Russ married Elizabeth Mae Francis. They had a daughter, Beth Francis on May 5th 1940 and a son Oran on July 20th 1942. He and his wife built a house in Plattsville and lived there until 1983 when they moved into an apartment in Kitchener.

Before the war Russ worked at Canada Sand and when he was discharged he went back to them for a while but decided to try his hand at construction with Dumfries Construction out of Galt. They were laying sewer pipes in cities in Ontario. He then went with Nadrofsky Steel in Brantford. He had his crane operator's license and operated their big machines. Some Native Canadians were outstanding in high steel work so many of his fellow workers were from the Brantford area. After nineteen years Lackie Brothers, also a steel erection company in Kitchener, hired Russ as a superintendent. He was involved in building Moose Factory on Hudson Bay, installing the water system in the top of the C.N. Tower and erecting several of the bridges on 401 Highway. He also spent three years in New Brunswick installing environmental protection systems in pulp and paper mills. Russ retired from Lackie Brothers in 1983 at 66 years of age.

He and his wife bought a 15 foot trailer and enjoyed travelling around the country and eventually graduated to one of the largest. They set it up in a park near Kitchener and spent most of their summers in it.

Russ died on January 19th 1997.

FLEMING Andrew Murray

Andrew was born on October 24th 1922 in Poole. After graduating from High School he joined the Fighting Perth Regiment out of Stratford in November 1939. The regiment was posted to Camp Borden for training. They were then sent to Niagara Falls to guard the hydro power plant, after that it was back to Borden for further training.

The Regiment was sent overseas and disembarked at Liverpool on October 17th 1941. They were taken to Chilton Foliat, Farnham in Surrey, Aldershot and the Brighton Hove area for further training. They took more specialized training at Barton Stacey and Eastbourne before shipping out from Liverpool on October 27th 1943 for Italy. The Perths arrived at Naples on November 8th 1943. After a year of constant fighting they shipped out of Florence on February 22nd 1945 to Marseilles. They went by train to Belgium and fought their way through to Defzijl where the war ended on the 8th of May 1945.

Shipped back to Canada Andrew was discharged in September 1945. He got a job at the Feed Mill in New Hamburg and married Loretta Stere on March 21st 1946. They had a big family. Andrew John was born on August 17th 1946. William Murray arrived on November 29th 1948, followed by Robert Daniel on January 28th 1950. Then followed four girls, Debra Lee was born on October 26th 1952 and she was joined by Barbara Ellen on September 12th 1954 followed by Patricia Diane on November 10th 1955. Marjorie Jane was the final daughter born on March 25th 1957. Ronald David was the next boy born on June 26th 1959 followed by Kevin Michael on October 4th 1960. Clare James completed the family on November 11th 1961.

The family moved to Plattsville and then Bright where Andrew set up his own roofing business. After he retired he suffered from poor health and moved into the Peoples Care Nursing Home in Tavistock.

Andrew died on April 27th 1996.

FOREMAN David George   Serv. # 868440

David was born on April 4th 1898 in Gilbert Plains, Manitoba to Mr. and Mrs. John Foreman. He worked on his father's farm near Bright, Ontario until he joined the army on April 15th 1917. David was 5 feet 10 inches tall. His chest girth when fully expanded was 40 1/2 inches and the range of expansion was 3 1/2 inches He was of medium complexion with blue eyes and brown hair. He also had a scar on the back of his left hand and a small scar on his right knee. David served overseas with the 4th Battalion of the Canadian Expeditionary Force (C.E.F.) and was badly wounded in September of 1918. He died of his wounds on the 29th of September.

FRIED John Carl

John was born on May 15th 1920 to Ephriam and Edna Fried. In 1935 he had to leave school to work at home on the farm. In January 1942 Jack joined the Army Service Corps. He was assigned to driving trucks attached to the Medium Artillery. He went overseas in June 1942 in a convoy. Jack was on the Empress of Japan. The transport drivers trained in England until D-Day. Jack was posted to France ten days after D-Day. He transported shells to the medium artillery batteries using Mack Trucks. The shells weighed in at 90 lbs. each and Jack took 220 in a load. He followed the guns through France, Belgium and Holland.

When the war ended Jack was utilized to pull our tanks out of Germany. He finally finished and was sent home in January 1946. Jack received his honourable discharge in February 1946. He went back to agricultural work on his father's farm.

On March 29th, 1947 Jack married Doris Cameron Marshall, the smartest thing he ever did. In April 1947 he got a farm under Veterans Land Act. Two years later they started a family. William Terry, the first child, was born on March 3rd 1949. Cathryn Ann then came along on May 31st 1950. Ronald Zack followed on November 24th 1951. The next brother, Brian Russell didn't show up until December 21st 1957 and Jamie Douglas appeared on January 12th 1959. Laurie May completed the family on March 8th 1961.

Jack and Doris, as of 2003, still live on the farm which their son operates.

FULCHER Alvin C.   Serv. #   R145777

Alvin was born on April 19th 1921 to Mr. and Mrs Charles Fulcher of Plattsville. He joined the Royal Canadian Air Force (R.C.A.F.) in January 1942. After Manning Depot in Toronto he was posted to Fredericton, New Brunswick and then Clinton, Ontario where he studied as a Radio Technician and was involved in secret radar and navigation techniques. In August of 1942 he was posted overseas and was stationed at a radar station in England on secret flying navigation systems. Alvin received his discharge in September 1945.

He married Margaret Prince. They had three children, Beth Donovan, Helen Mitchner and Leslie.

Alvin died on June 8th 1999.

FULCHER Roy Everett   Serv.# R183745

Roy was born on May 26th 1924, the son of Mr. and Mrs. Charles Fulcher.

He took his entire schooling in Plattsville and earned the Top Student Award at his High School graduation in June of 1942. He joined the Royal Canadian Air Force (R.C.A.F.) in September 1942. He was posted to Manning Depot in Toronto, then to Aylmer for Initial Training School. His next course was at Navigation Training School in Malton. He graduated on October 14th 1943, received his navigator wings and was promoted to Sergeant. He was posted overseas on October 31st 1943 and after further training joined #189 Squadron on Lancasters and was promoted to Warrant Officer 2nd Class. He was reported missing on February 2 1945 during a night bombing raid on Karlsruhe. Roy was 20 years of age. On July 26th 1945 his family received word that he was presumed dead. His name is inscribed on both the Cenotaph in Victoria Park in Woodstock and the Cenotaph in Chesterfield.

Roy is buried in the Dumbach War Cemetery in Germany.

Chesterfield Cenotaph

GOFF Harry William Serv.# A-56879

Harry was born on October 16th 1918 in Bright, Ontario to Frank and Mary Goff. After finishing school he did agricultural work on his father's farm and other farms in the area. He enlisted in the Canadian Army on the 20th of September 1941 in Kitchener, Ontario. He served in Canada and Britain. Harry received an honourable discharge on June 3rd 1946. He received the Canadian Volunteer Service Medal with Clasp and the War Medal 1939-45.

After the war Harry did agricultural work for a while working on his father's farm. In 1946 he went on a harvest excursion to Saskatchewan and then went on to Vancouver. He apprenticed as a carpenter with McKinney Lumber Company. He came back to Woodstock, Ontario in late 1948 and started constructing houses.

On March 14th 1953 Harry married Francis Elinor Copeland. In 1957 Harry formed Goff Construction Ltd. and expanded to building not only single family houses, but also duplexes and apartment buildings. His favourite recreations were lawn bowling and curling.

Francis and Harry had a daughter Shirley Elizabeth born on December 12th 1954. She went to Western in London and got her degree as a Chartered Accountant. On May 18th 1991 she married Judson Martin. Shirley still manages Goff Construction Ltd.

Francis lives in Woodstock and Harry is in the hospital in London in 2003.

GRAHAM Blair Alexander   Serv. # R-68401

Blair was born on October 20th 1918. After finishing school he worked in his father's hardware store in Bright. In April of 1940 Blair joined the Royal Canadian Air Force (R.C.A.F.) and was posted to St. Thomas to learn aero-engine maintenance. On completion of his course he was posted to #12 Service Flying Training School in Brandon, Manitoba in the early part of 1941. On May 17th 1941 Margaret Routly and Blair were married in Brandon, Manitoba. Shortly after he was posted to the Queen Charlotte Islands in British Columbia to a Coastal Command Station. After a few months here he was posted to Ketchecan in Alaska. The Squadron flew Catalina flying boats. Shortly after Victory in Japan (V. J.) Day Blair was sent back to Ontario and received his discharge. Blair then went into a partnership with his brother and father in the Hardware Store in Bright.

On August 13th 1945 a daughter Betty Ann was born. James Everett followed on March 18th 1948, and Joan Elizabeth completed the family on October 18th 1950. Blair was an avid hunter and fisherman and enjoyed baseball and hockey. Over the next few years he built his own cottage north of Temiskaming on Grindstone Lake. Blair was appointed by the Federal Department of Agriculture as an Inspector of agricultural produce in the early fifties. He sold the Hardware Store in 1982, but continued with the Agricultural Department till 1988. He and Margaret spent many happy days at their cottage.

Blair died on October 6th 1996, just short of his 78th birthday. Margaret followed on December 6th 1997.

GREEN John Stewart

Stewart was born on September 28th 1922 to Sidney Allen and Elizabeth Stewart Green. When he completed his schooling he went to work at Canada Sand. In July of 1942 Stewart joined the Royal Canadian Air Force (R.C.A.F.) and was posted to Manning Depot in Toronto. He then took Initial Training School in Calgary followed by Bombing and Gunnery School. He graduated from Fingal, Alberta in September of 1943 after completing his Wireless Course as a W.A.G. (Wireless Air Gunner). He was posted to the Bahamas to fly in Coastal Command searching the Atlantic Ocean for submarines. He was fortunate to be entertained by the Duke of Windsor, who at that time was the Governor General of the Bahamas. He completed a tour of duty and in March of 1944 was posted to England and then Northern Ireland where he and his crew completed another tour. He was promoted to Flying Officer while on this tour. Stewart arrived home on August 12th 1945. He received his honourable discharge in September of 1945.

He returned to work at Canada Sand and on July the 15th 1946 he married Jean Hagelstein. They had two daughters. Judith Ann was born on April 11th 1948 followed by Susan Margaret on July 30th 1952.

Carborundum Abrasives, an American firm, bought Canada Sand and in 1960 they transferred Stewart to one of their plants in Germany. He was there for two and a half years. They then transferred him to their plant in Niagara Falls, New York. They left Stewart there until 1970 when they sent him to another plant in Lebanon, Indiana. Stewart retired in 1987 and he and his wife remained in Lebanon.

Stewart died on the 15th of January 1998.

GREEN Sidney Allen Service # 452682

Sidney was born to John Collis and Sarah Alice Green on November 18th 1892 on a farm in Wilmot Township. The family moved to a farm in Blenheim Township shortly after his birth.

He attended school on the 10th Concession and helped on the farm. Sidney and his brother James operated a cider mill for two years. Later they bought a planing mill in Plattsville. Sidney joined the army on October 18th 1917. He was 5 feet 1 1/2 inches tall. His chest girth was 36 inches when fully expanded and had a range of expansion of 2 inches. He had a fair complexion with blue eyes and light brown hair. He served overseas in France and was gassed.

After the war he came back to Plattsville and worked at the McKie Buggy Works. On September 28th 1921 he married Elizabeth Stewart Hall. They had a son, John Stewart, on September 28th 1922. Sydney then bought a truck and transported furniture for the factory in Plattsville. He later worked for Canada Sand and remained with them until he retired.

Sidney died on May 3rd 1977.

Sidney is fourth from the left in the second row.

GRIEVE James Douglas

Douglas was born in Plattsville on March 19th 1915 to Elizabeth and James Grieve. After leaving school in the early thirties he worked at Canada Sand Paper. Douglas and Nellie Evelyn Ellis, the daughter of Oliver Ellis, were secretly married on August 28th 1937 in Niagara Falls, New York. Douglas had Bright's disease but wanted to join the navy. He switched his urine sample with a friend when he enlisted so the Bright's disease was not detected and he was accepted into the navy in 1941. He did not disclose his marriage and sent a portion of his pay to his mother. He was stationed in London, Toronto, Halifax and later Newfoundland on shore duty. He was a leading Supply Assistant in Newfoundland. In the navy he was diagnosed with Bright's disease, so on his discharge was awarded a pension. He went back to work at Canada Sand and continued to partially support his mother.

Douglas died in January 1953.

GRIMES Donald Ronald

Donald was born in Philadelphia, Pennsylvania on July 14th 1922. In July 1940 he enlisted in the Royal Canadian Air Force (R.C.A.F.) and was sent to Winnipeg for Manning Depot. In February of 1941 he was posted to Galt Aircraft School and in July that year he was posted to Winnipeg as a Leading Aircraftsman in aero-engine mechanics. After further training in Calgary, Montreal and Dorval, Don graduated as a Flight Engineer in late 1943. He was posted to Gander in Newfoundland and then Torbay as a Flight Engineer on Coastal Command. He flew in Catalinas and then the B24 Liberator. Don received his honourable discharge from the Air Force on September 29th 1945.

Samuel Bert Grimes, Don's father, started Canada Sand in Plattsville around 1930 so it was natural that Donald went to work in the family firm after his discharge from the air force as he had worked there before joining up. On March 15th 1947 Don married Effie Romaniuk (Ronnie) from the Yorkton area of Saskatchewan. They had one son Garth Emery born on May 19th 1965. Carborundum bought out Canada Sand and in 1950 they sent Don to Niagara Falls, New York to manage their plant there. In 1953, he was sent to another plant in South Carolina and then Atlanta, Georgia for six months.

Don finally left Carborundum in 1959 and started Grimes Abrasives in Newmarket. Although it is no longer in the family Grimes Abrasives is now headquartered in Toronto and Don is still very well thought of by the new owners.

Donald died on May 24th 1994.

GRIMES James Keith

Jim was born on May 22nd 1933 to Kenneth and Maggie Grimes in Plattsville. After finishing school he went to work in construction. In June 1951 Jim joined the army and was sent to Currie Barracks in Calgary for training. He was posted to the Royal Canadian Regiment and sent to Korea in August of 1952. Jim was wounded three times in Korea and had to be hospitalized each time. He was finally sent home in the summer of 1953. James received his honourable discharge in late 1953.

Jim returned to Plattsville and went back to construction work. In 1956 his father was sent to Australia to set up a new plant for Carborundum Abrasives. In November 1961 Jim decided to join him. He went into construction work in Australia and in February 1962 he married Dierdre McCarthy, a whirlwind courtship for sure. They adopted an Aboriginal son, James, in 1966. He is now a detective and in 2002 still lives at home. In 1968 they adopted a daughter Catherine who also still lives at home. Jim and his family live in Rossmore about 40 miles from Sydney.

GRIMES Philip Mason   Serv.# R-89403

Philip was born in Augusta, Maine on August 23rd 1920. His parents were Warren and Ruth Grimes. After completing school Philip went to work at Canada Sand, which his Grandfather, Samuel Bert Grimes started in Plattsville with Earl Stark and P.R. Hilborn from Preston. In August of 1940 Philip joined the Royal Canadian Air Force (R.C.A.F.) and was posted to Galt Aircraft School. He served as a Leading Aircraftsman in the R.C.A.F for 5 years. He was stationed at Dunnville. In October 1943 he was sent overseas and attached to #427 Squadron, the Lion Squadron, in Yorkshire England. While in Dunnville Philip married Elizabeth Ann Romaniuk and a son William Warren was born in May of 1943. On December 15th 1945 Philip received his honourable discharge and rejoined Canada Sand.

John Robert, the second son, was born on August 9th 1949. Shortly after Carborundum Abrasives bought out Canada Sand. Philip was sent on a technical assignment to the Carborundum factory in Brazil for six weeks. Following this he was appointed as a product engineer at the main plant in Niagara Falls, New York. In 1959 he left Carborundum to join his brothers in Grimes Abrasives in Newmarket. However, Carborundum wanted him to go to Australia and set up a new factory so in 1960 he rejoined them and went to Australia for three years. After this project was successfully completed Carborundum made him Technical Manager travelling the world to oversee all Carborundum plants.

Philip retired in 1995 but continued with some consulting work. He now, in 2003, resides in Keswick, Ontario.

Harvey Blackmore   Donald Grimes   Philip Grimes

GRIMES Thelma

Thelma was born on August 9th 1924 to Warren and Ruth Grimes. She joined the Canadian Women's Army Corps on January 6th 1944. She served 1 year and 2 months as a private. She was stationed at Kitchener, Toronto and Halifax. Thelma was married to James Charles Steele from Woodstock on November 25th 1944. Jim was in The Royal Canadian Navy. Thelma was honourably discharged on March 1st 1945. Jim, after his discharge, was employed in Customs and Excise in Woodstock.

Thelma and Jim had two children. James David was born on December 11th 1945 and Nora Louise on June 15th 1948. Jim retired from Customs and Excise in 1985 and they, as of 2003, are still happily residing in Woodstock.

HABERMEHL Albert Leroy

Roy was born on January 6th 1925 to William and Merle Habermehl. Immediately after finishing school in 1941 he joined the army at 16 years of age. On February 6th 1943 he married Doris Alma Hart. Roy volunteered for the Paratroops and was sent to Fort Benning in Georgia where he earned his wings as a Paratrooper. He then joined the Devil's Brigade Paraskiers in Helena, Montana. This was an elite unit that was half Canadian and half American. He was badly injured in a training accident. This turned out to be a lucky accident as the unit subsequently jumped into Italy and were wiped out. Roy was posted to Camp Borden as a weapons instructor. He later joined the Essex Scottish Regiment who were posted to England. They landed in France in September 1944. Roy was wounded on October 5th near Antwerp while under heavy shellfire. His right hand and shoulder were badly mangled, and the right hand had to be amputated at the wrist. On December 22nd three plane loads of wounded were flown back to England. Roy had been transferred to the plane with mainly Canadians. The other two planes crashed and all were killed. Roy received his honourable discharge in late 1945.

Roy and Doris had four children. Diane Doris was born on December 27th 1944. Allan Roy was next on January 26th 1949. Edward Ray followed on February 10th 1950 and Robin Reid completed the family on January 4th 1954.

Roy was hired as Deputy Clerk of Galt after his discharge. Shortly after he was appointed as Town Clerk of Preston where he served for thirty years. He then was made First Clerk of Cambridge until his retirement in January 1981. Roy also served as Secretary Treasurer of the War Amps for many years.

Roy died on September 22nd 1992.

HALL Donald Andrew   Serv. # 112285

Donald was born on July 19th 1926 in Paris, Ontario. His parents were David and Jean Hall. He joined the Army on January 3rd 1945 in London, Ontario and took his basic training at Chatham, Ontario and advanced training at Ipperwash. Donald was slated for Pacific duty, but Victory in Japan (V.J.) Day cancelled any need for that. He received his discharge on April 16th 1946. After his discharge Donald went on to University for 3 years and then returned to the family farm.

On September 6th 1952 he married Gloria Margaret Elizabeth Abernethy. They had six children. Bryan Donald was born on October 6th 1953. Gary Stephen arrived on April 18th 1956. Robert Douglas was next on January 22nd 1959. The first girl, Jennifer Helen, made her debut on December 28th 1962 followed by a sister Dianne Elizabeth on January 18th 1966. Darren Jeffrey completed the family on May 6th 1969. Gary and Jennifer were tragically killed in accidents, Gary on October 18th 1963 and Jennifer on April 10th 1970.

In 1958 Donald took over the family farm and has operated it ever since. In 2002, Donald and Gloria celebrated their 50th Wedding Anniversary.

50th Anniversary

Donald and Gloria Hall
ld and Gloria Hall of RR 4, Bright will celebrate their
anniversary on September 6, 2002.
Love and best wishes from your family

HALL Douglas Gemmell   Serv. # A114417

Douglas was born on September 13th 1919 in Bright. His parents were Morton and Elizabeth (Bessie) Hall. After completing school Doug worked in agriculture until he joined the Canadian Army on December 8th 1941. After basic and advanced training Doug was posted to the west coast and served there until his discharge in late 1945.

Doug came back to Plattsville and worked on his parents farm until the late 1940's when he took it over.

Douglas died in 1982. Robert Hall took over the farm.

HALL G. Perry

Perry was born in 1893 to Stephen Hall Jr. and his wife Clara (nee-Cumming). He received his honourable discharge in 1919 with the rank of Captain.

In the twenties Perry and a brother operated an automobile agency out of the old McKie Buggy Factory in Plattsville. In 1927 Perry, a brother and Percy McKie formed a company, Hall and McKie Ltd. and operated a Ford dealership in Kitchener for a number of years.

Perry died in 1953.

HALL Henry Richard Serv.# 2365914

Plattsville Memorial Gates

Henry was born on March 28th 1897 to John and Elizabeth Hall in Plattsville. Henry joined the army on August 2nd 1918. He was 21 years of age, 5 feet 8 inches in height and his chest when fully expanded was 37 inches with a range of expansion of 5 inches. Henry had a fair complexion with gray eyes and brown hair.

HALL James Graham

James was born on August 13th 1901 to John R. and Ida Jean (nee-Graham) Hall on the family farm just south of Plattsville on the 12th Concession. After completing school Jim obtained work in agriculture on the home farm and at other farms in the area. In the late thirties he obtained employment at the Brantford Coach and Body Works in Brantford.

He joined the militia in Brantford and took a course at the Royal Canadian School of Artillery in Kingston as a Bombardier. He was posted overseas in July of 1941 with the 16th Guelph Battery. His unit was shipped to France right after the invasion. They fought through France, Belgium and Holland and wound up in Wilhelmshaven in Germany. On January 6th 1946 Jim married Jessie Catherine Griggs in England. He returned to Canada in late 1946 and received his honourable discharge. He obtained employment with J.D. Adams Co. in Paris who made very large heavy equipment.

The family moved to Paris at this time. The family started while he was still in the army. David James was born on September 23rd 1946. Daphne Jayne followed on October 23rd 1949 and Stephen Graham completed the family on January 16th 1959.

Jim retired in 1966 at 65 years of age. He died on March 11th 1977.

HALLMAN Gordon   Serv. # A-108261

Gordon was born on June 24th 1924 in Toronto. He joined the army in early 1943. He was placed in the Engineers. They were trained to do all manner of construction for the army. They constructed fortifications, built bridges both solid and temporary pontoon and any other construction work necessary for the infantry, artillery and armoured corps. He was at Ipperwash when he was sent overseas in late 1943. He served in Britain, France, Belgium and Holland. Gord was sent home and received his honourable discharge at the end of 1945. He was awarded the 1939-45 Star, the Canadian Volunteer Service Medal and Clasp and the War Medal 1939-45.

Gord went to work at Leigh Instruments in Kitchener. On September 23rd 1950 he married Eileen Bast. They had four children. Paul Gordon was born on June 21st 1951. Paulette Grace came next on July 12th 1953, Dennis Keith arrived on January 19th 1957 and Dale Murray completed the family on June 3rd 1958.

In 1954 Gordon and Eileen moved to Plattsville with their family. Gord went with Com Dev in Cambridge. He became very active in the Boy Scouts in Plattsville and was eventually awarded a 30 year service pin. He also became an Assistant Commissioner of the Scouts. He loved camping and the family spent time every summer enjoying this form of recreation. Gord was a very tall man at six feet five inches.

Gordon died on October 4th 2000.

HALLMAN Peter Gordon   Serv.# V-92555

Peter was born on February 9th 1925 to Clarence and Jean Hallman. He went to Elementary School at Blink Bonnie and Secondary at Plattsville Continuation School graduating in the spring of 1942. He went to Stratford Normal School for his teaching certificate and then taught at the Hallman School two miles north of Washington for the 1943-44 school year.

On October 2nd 1944 Peter joined the Royal Canadian Navy in London, Ontario. He served in Halifax, Shelburne and near Digby, all in Nova Scotia. He was discharged shortly after Victory in Japan (V.J.) and went to University on the Veterans program. He achieved an Honours B.A. in Business Administration.

Peter married Marjorie Alice Bean on December 26th 1950. They had four children. Wendy Jean started the family on June 28th 1955 followed by Mark Robert on July 17th 1956. John Gordon joined on May 15th 1959 and Heather Louise completed the family on September 15th 1964.

After completing University Peter went with Kresges. Some time later he joined Northern Life. After a time he decided to go it alone and bought an Insurance Agency in Galt. He turned the business over to his sons in 1995 to enjoy a life of leisure. In 2003 Peter is still enjoying a well deserved retirement with his wife Marjorie.

HALLMAN Russell Clarence

Russell was born on July 7th 1920. When he finished school he worked on the home farm until October 1st 1940 when he attended a wireless and morse code school for the military in Guelph. On completion of the course in March 1941 Russell volunteered for the navy and took further training in Toronto. In September the navy contingent marched in the last C.N.E. parade until the end of the war. Early October 1941 Russ was posted to H.M.C.S. Stadacona in Halifax. Shortly after he was sent to Sorel in Quebec to pick up a new Corvette to be taken to Lunenburg for outfitting and guns. Naturally it was christened H.M.C.S. Lunenburg.

On February 14th 1942 Russell married Isabel Baird. He studied Azdic and was posted to the Corvette H.M.C.S Camrose where he was mailman and Azdic operator. At the end of 1942 they were on convoy to England in the worst storm in a century. They had to shut down the engines as the bearings overheated. Fortunately the Captain was very capable and swung the ship around to run with the storm. Waves were upwards of fifty feet and they would have foundered if he had been unsuccessful. A tug came out and towed them to St. Johns for repairs. They then guarded a convoy to England and wound up in Londonderry where Russ had a tiddily suit made. The material was far superior to issue and the tailoring superb. Then it was back to Halifax for a dose of the mumps.

Russell served on the Brandon and Baddeck after the Camrose. Some Corvettes were given closed Fo'c's'le (forecastle) decks. They were more comfortable, but also increased casualties in case of sinking. Russ ran with 6 convoys to England, was twice on the Murmansk run, which was the most dangerous and arduous duty in the navy. They took 4 merchant ships to Algeria in the summer of 1943. They also sailed down the west coast of Africa and had a trip to Iceland. Russel came home at the end of August and was given his honourable discharge in October of 1945. He was awarded the Canadian Volunteer Service Medal and Clasp, The Atlantic Star, The Africa Star and the War Service Medal with Oak Leaf.

Isabel and Russ had four children. Russell Baird was born on July 6th 1943. Ruth Isabel checked in on March 29th 1946, another son, Peter John arrived on March 1st 1950. Susan Jean completed the family on August 30th 1952.

Under the Veterans Land Act (V.L.A.) Russ bought the old Hogarth farm three miles west of Bright and in 2003 lives there still.

HAMACHER Allan Duncan   Serv. # 164100

Allan D. Hamacher   Pte   Killed Nov. 22nd/911

Allan was born on August 12th 1891 in Bright to Allan Sylvester and Sarah Ellen (nee-Nellie) Hamacher. Allan was a farm worker and joined the army on September 2nd, 1915. He was 5 feet 4 inches tall with a chest girth of 35 inches when fully expanded. He was of fair complexion and hair with light blue eyes. Allan had two scars on his left thigh.

Allan was killed in action on the 22nd of November 1916 while serving as a Private with the 73rd Battalion, Royal Highlanders of Canada. He has no known grave, but his name is inscribed on the Vimy Ridge Memorial and the Chesterfield Cenotaph. His picture is hung in the Bright Church and is reproduced here.

They Died for King and Country

FRED VEITCH
HERBERT CHRISTMAS
THOS. ADCOCK
LINDSAY HASTINGS
ALLAN HAMACHER
JOHN CRERAR
ROY ELLIS
HAROLD FRASER
JOHN B. WILLSON
CLIFFORD BROWN
GORDON STAUFFER
A. R. BUSH

In Loving Memory of

Private A. D. Hamacher, who died for his King and Country, on November 22nd, 1916.

Servant of God, well done!
  Thy glorious warfare's past;
The battle's fought, the victory won
  And thou art crowned at last

Soldier of Christ, well done!
  Praise be thy new employ;
And, while eternal ages run,
  Rest in thy Saviour's joy

—Parents and Family

HAMACHER Alvin Duncan

Alvin was born August 12th 1881 to Allan and Sarah Ellen Hamacher in Plattsville. After completing school Alvin went to British Columbia to work in forestry. He joined the 231st Battalion of the Canadian Expeditionary Force (C.E.F.) on the 17th of October 1916 in Vancouver. He served in France and this picture of him was taken in Plattsville on August 11th 1919. Alvin was honourably discharged shortly after. He went back to British Columbia and worked on a farm in Ladner. Some time later he worked for Buckerfields in Vancouver installing incubators and brooders in chicken farms.

On March 11th 1928 Alvin married Sonja Evelina Johnson who was born in Sweden. They had three children, Gilbert, who was killed at age 16 in a saw mill accident, Alvin Eric was born on January 22nd 1929 and Barbara May was born in 1937.

Alvin died in 1972.

HAMACHER Arthur Duncan

Arthur was born on May 12th 1899 to Allan and Sarah Ellen (Nelly) Hamacher in Plattsville. When he left school he worked in agriculture till the end of the First World War when he went out to British Columbia and began life as a prospector. In the winters he did landscaping. He joined the forces early in the Second World War and was duly posted to England. While there he met and married Ivy Mellor of Manchester. She was twenty two years his junior, but they both loved dancing and were an excellent match. When the war ended they settled in Kitchener. Arthur built a Quonset hut home and did landscaping and also worked for the city. He had a wonderful sense of humour. He told a relative that he had a great job with the city and had hundreds under him at work. This was absolutely true as he was caretaker of the cemetery.

Arthur and Ivy wasted no time in starting a family. Thomas Harold was born on January 9th 1947. Janice May followed on February 15th 1948. As the family grew Art built a bigger home on his lot to accommodate the new family members. When Gordon Arthur joined the family on October 26th 1952 they all moved into the new house. The last son, Gregory Allan, made his debut on October 16th 1958. Patricia Gay was born on March 22nd, 1962 and Lorraine Elizabeth arriving on February 9th 1966 completed the family.

Arthur died of heart trouble on February 23rd 1966 shortly after the birth of Lorraine leaving a very young family. He is buried in the Woodlawn cemetery.

HAMACHER Gordon Boyd

Gordon was born on September 9th, 1907 in Blenheim Township to Allan and Sarah Ellen Hamacher. He was raised and went to school in Plattsville. He went with his father on harvest excursions to Western Canada. His father was a horseman and raised stallions. After finishing school Gordon got a job with Hay and Company in Woodstock. They ran a lumber mill and some time later Allen bought his own truck and hauled logs from the north country to the mill.

Gordon joined the army in the London District Depot on February 18th 1942. He was a Gunner in the Artillery and served in Canada, the United Kingdom and Europe. He volunteered for the Pacific but Victory in Japan (V.J.) Day finished that, and also delayed his discharge to April 3rd 1946.

Gordon returned to Plattsville and went to work at Canada Sand. On June 30th 1948 he married Donna Blanche Edwards in the Plattsville United Church. They had one son, Michael, born on July 8th 1949. Gord suffered from ill health, and after a breakdown retired from Canada Sand in 1964.

Gordon died on October 10th 1972 in the Plattsville he always loved.

HARMER Albert Lyle

Lyle was born on August 19th 1898 in Plattsville to Albert and Keziah Harmer. His father worked in the local furniture factory and after finishing school Lyle apprenticed as a carpenter. He joined the Canadian Expeditionary Force (C.E.F) on May 9th 1917.

Lyle was 5 feet 4 1/2 inches tall with a chest girth of 37 inches and a range of expansion of 3 1/2 inches. He had a fair complexion, blue eyes and fair hair. He was a Methodist. Lyle served overseas and was shipped home in 1919. He received his honourable discharge in the fall of 1919. Lyle emigrated to the United States after the war, married and lived in Toledo, Ohio.

HARMER Jacky Ray Ervin   Serv.# A-82039

Jack was born on April 27th 1920. When he was 14 years old he started to deliver bread for Scott Brothers Bakery in Plattsville. They delivered to all the farms in the area. They offered him a job as a driver so Jacky hied himself off to Woodstock and by a little finessing of the birth facts got his drivers license. Jack joined the Oxford Rifles in 1940. He took training in London, Camp Borden, Prince George and Debert, Nova Scotia. After an embarkation leave Jack was shipped overseas in February 1943. For a time he was attached to the Essex Scottish. He was posted to the Royal Canadian Regiment and went into the Sicily fighting with them. While in Sicily he was transferred to the Anti-Tank Corps and was among the first to land in Italy. In October 1944 Jack was wounded by shrapnel. He was sent to a hospital in Rome and then transferred to London, England. The Doctors in London were going to amputate his leg, but fortunately his brother was there and objected vociferously. A Canadian Doctor listened and agreed. Jacky spent nine months in hospital recuperating. Jack was Mentioned in Dispatches for the engagement in which he was wounded and also for his work in the Anti-Tank Corps. Jack was discharged in late 1945.

After his discharge in 1945 Jack got a job at Newlands Textiles in Cambridge. Jacky and Margaret Thomson were married on December 7th 1946. They had four children. Margaret Ann was born on December 5th 1947 but tragically died on November 3rd 1948. Jack and James were born on July 28th 1950. James was still born. Another son, Donald, was born on November 28th 1952. Jacky worked at Newlands until he retired at 65 years of age.

Jacky died on January 18th 2000.

HARMER Gerald D'arcy Strome   Serv.# R90206

Jay was born on March 17th, 1915 and on completion of Senior Matric at Continuation School went to work for Canada Sand. He joined the Royal Candian Air Force (R.C.A.F.) in 1940 at 25 years of age where he served 4 1/2 years. He was stationed in London, Toronto, Jarvis, and Victoriaville, Quebec where he took Initial Training School. He took his Elementary Flying Training School in Nova Scotia and Service Flying Training in Moncton, New Brunswick. At Trenton he was remustered and sent to Regina on a course. He was posted to Edmonton and then Halifax for a year, he was promoted to the rank of Sergeant. He spent time in Lachine, Quebec and Maitland, Nova Scotia before being sent to McGill University to study research in Aviation medicine. At the completion of that course he was posted to Debert, Nova Scotia where he served as in instructor in night vision and high altitude work. While in the service he applied for permission to marry. On May 15th 1943 Flying Officer E. J. McClusky wrote Jay thus.

MEMORANDUM 22-4

To: R90206 Sgt. Harmer, G.D.

Permission to Marry:

1. Permission is hereby granted for you to be married to Miss Marjorie Hall of Ayr, Ontario, on or about June 19th 1943.
2. Upon your return to this unit, report the particulars to the Accounts section.
   Submit your Marriage Certificate for Copying, after which it will be returned to you.

E.J. McCluskey F.O.
Assistant Adjutant
Halifax, N.S.
May 15 1943

Following orders Jay married Marjorie Helen Hall on June 19th 1943 at Knox United Church in Ayr. They had a son, Dwight Jay, born on November 6th 1944. Fortunately Helen was a Registered Nurse as Dwight had severe medical problems. Jay received his honourable discharge in 1945 and rejoined Canada Sand. He and Marjorie had three more children, Joel Travis born on January 28th 1950 and Karen Ellen on July 16th 1951. Dwight died in April 1952. Gail Diane completed the family on September 17th 1952.

Jay died on February 2nd 1971.

HARVEY Arthur Gow Serv.# J-86594

Gow was born on December 26th 1923 to Robert and Lois Harvey in Roblin, Manitoba. On January 8th 1942 he joined the Royal Canadian Air Force (R.C.A.F) in Winnipeg, Manitoba and was shipped to Manning Depot at Lachine, Quebec. At the end of February he was sent to Moncton, New Brunswick for guard duty. The beginning of May he was posted to Victoriaville, Quebec for Initial Training School. He contracted mumps and was hospitalized. At the end of July he graduated and was sent to Air Observers School in Ancienne, Lorette just outside Quebec City. At completion of the course graduation day for the class was November the 6th. Gow received his navigator wing and was promoted to Sergeant. The class was given two weeks embarkation leave and on December 12th they sailed for England out of Halifax on the Queen Elizabeth, the largest and fastest ship afloat. They were told there were 25,000 military personnel aboard, but some doubted the number. On the 18th of December they docked at Greenock for a train ride to No. 3 Personnel Reception Centre at Bournemouth.

On January 29th 1943 Gow was posted to Desford near Leicester, flying Tiger Moths for map reading. Then his group was posted to Dumfries in Scotland for Advanced Flying Unit (A.F.U.), flying in Ansons. They were then posted to Pershore for Operational Training Unit on Wellington bombers. They were put into flight crews and after graduation were sent to Conversion unit in Wombleton, Yorkshire. Here they flew Halifax Mark 11's and had a mid-upper gunner and flight engineer added to each crew. At the end of December his crew were posted to 431 Squadron at Croft in Yorkshire.

On February 20th 1944 they were shot down by a night fighter during a raid on Leipzig. Gow was the only member of the crew that survived. After capture and interrogation at Dulag Luft a group of prisoners were loaded on cattle cars and shipped to Stalag Luft 6 at Hydekrug in East Prussia, about 20 miles from Memel Lithuania. There were 60 men to a hut with no heat and double wooden bunks with bed boards. A straw filled palliasse with two ersatz wool blankets completed the bed. On July 17th, because the Russians were too close, the Germans moved them to Stalag 357 near Thorne in Poland. Towards the end of August they were again loaded in cattle cars, 40 men in each end and six guards in the middle. Of course there was barbed wire fencing on each end of the box car. They were shipped by slow train to Falingsbostel near Hanover.

On Friday April 6th 1944 the Allied troops got too close and the prisoners were marched out of camp to the East, across the Elbe river and towards the Baltic Sea. In May they were finally liberated by a couple of Tommies and flown back to England from Lunenburg, Germany in Dakotas. Gow celebrated Victory in Europe (V.E.) Day in a hospital in Bramshott, England. He sailed for home the 7th of July on the Ile de France. It was great to be home. In due course he got his honourable discharge.

On December 20th 1958 Gow married Jennifer Ann Becks. They bought the old Cumming house one mile south of Washington in 1967 and have been active in the community ever since. They have two sons, Marcus Gow born on February 10th 1968 and Michael Gow born on July 29th 1971.

HASKELL Reginald

Reg was born on December 6th 1918 to Edgar and Beatrice Haskell. They lived just west of Chesterfield Church and Edgar was caretaker of the Church and Cemetery. Reginald attended Blink Bonnie Elementary School and completed his High School at Plattsville Continuation School. After graduation Reg did agricultural work in the area. In very early 1940 he joined the army and was posted to the Provo Corps. Reg was posted to England in 1941.

In early 1942 he had an accident on his motorbike and broke his leg. He was sent to the Canadian Military Hospital at Brixham and when he recovered went to Torquay on leave and met Blanche Ethel Lonsdale. Blanche was a conductor on a bus. Reg and Blanche fell in love and were married on February 9th 1944. After we invaded France Reg served on the continent for a spell. When the war ended he was shipped back to Canada and received his discharge in October 1945. Blanche arrived shortly after and Reg joined the Woodstock police force in late 1945. He joined the O.P.P. in November 1946. He served in several locations finally retiring with the rank of corporal in April 1977. After leaving the O.P.P. they continued to live in Belleville and Reg did court duty from 1977 to 1988.

Reg and Blanche had three children. Agnes Blanche was born on April 14th 1947. Marilyn Ann followed on April 27th 1950 and Dale Edward completed the family on June 3rd. 1956.

Reg died on December 23rd 2001.

HASTINGS James Lindsay   Serv.# 475875

James was born on November 24th 1884 to Alexander and Jennet (nee-Little) Hastings. He had two older sisters and two younger brothers. Their mother died when the oldest girl was 12. Naturally she assumed the role of mother so the children were always very close. Jim spent his early years on the home farm. It has always been called the Glen Lee farm and is situated on Lot 23 and part of Lot 24 on the North half of Concession 13, Blenheim Township. The farm is still in the Hastings name. As his brothers took over more responsibilities Jim started working at the Bright Cheese and Butter Mfg. Co. He also spent some time at the Dorchester cheese plant near London. During this period he went to Guelph College and became a cheese and butter maker. As he became well and favourably known in the trade he was hired by a dairy in Toronto. While there he took a course to become an inspector.

Jim was a faithful member of Chesterfield Presbyterian Church. He also was a member of the Masonic Lodge in Plattsville.

When the First World War broke out Jim thought as the oldest brother he should go, so he enlisted in the Princess Patricia Canadian Light Infantry on July 29th 1915. He was 5 feet 8 1/4 inches tall with a chest girth of 41 1/2 inches fully expanded with a range of expansion of 4 1/2 inches. He had a fair complexion, gray blue eyes and brown hair. After initial training in Canada he was sent overseas with 1800 other soldiers. After further training in England James was promoted to Corporal and the unit was shipped to the front in France and Belgium.

In one of his letters home he mentioned the terrible conditions in the trenches during the winter. The mud, rats and smell of death were appalling.

A friend had sent him a scarf. It helped to keep him warm during the day and he folded it for a pillow at night! One relief of the boredom was when a cat took refuge in their trench with her kittens.

James was killed at Courcelette in the Battle of the Somme on September 15th 1916. He was 32 years of age and has no known grave. His name is inscribed on the Vimy Ridge Memorial and on the Cenotaph at Chesterfield.

HENSON William Ernest   Serv. # 772148

Loos British Cemetery

Chesterfield Cenotaph

William was born on April 3rd 1892 to Fred and Sarah Ann Henson, of 11 Northampton Road, in Wellingsborough, Northamptonshire, England. He emigrated to Canada in 1912 and worked for John Sillers of Ratho for three years. On October 20th 1915 Bill enlisted in the 125th Brant Dragoons. He was 5 feet 6 1/4 inches tall with a chest girth of 37 inches when fully expanded. His range of expansion was 2 1/4 inches He had a dark complexion, blue eyes and dark hair. Bill was a member of the Church of England.

William was killed in action on July 26th 1917 while fighting with the 1st Battalion of the C.E.F. He is buried in the Loos British Cemetery in France grave #550 and his name is inscribed on the Cenotaph in Chesterfield.

HILDERLY Edith May

Edith was born on June 5th 1921 on the family farm near Innerkip to John and Bessie Hilderly. She joined the Canadian Women's Army Corps in September 1943 in London, Ontario. After basic training she was posted to Kitchener and promoted to the rank of corporal. Edith received her honourable discharge in April of 1945. On March 6th 1945 she married Rudy J. Schmuck, a member of the Royal Canadian Air Force (R.C.A.F.).

Rudy was involved in telecommunications in the Air Force and continued in that work after his discharge in Winnipeg. He retired from that field in 1967 and they moved to Kelowna. In 1969 Rudy started working for the Post Office as a letter carrier. He continued with them until he retired in 1982.

In 2003 Edith and Rudy are still enjoying their retirement.

Edith and brother Russell

HILDERLY Russell John

Russell was born on July 4th 1925. After finishing his schooling Russell went to work at Canada Sand on July 2nd 1941. On March 10th 1944 he left Canada Sand to join the army in London, Ontario in the Army Service Corps. He was posted to Cornwall for basic training and Red Deer, Alberta for advanced training. Russell was then posted to Longeiul near Montreal to work in the stores, then to Debert, Nova Scotia in the Infantry Training Battalion of the Canadian Infantry Corps. He served there until his discharge in July 17th 1946. After his discharge he went back to his job at Canada Sand.

Russell married Hilda Freda Balewski on May 19th 1945. They had two sons, Brian Russell, born on July 25th 1962 and Bradley John born on September 5th 1965. Russell retired from Canada Sand on July 15th 1990 at sixty five years of age.

In 2003 Russell and Hilda reside in Roseville.

HILDERLY Robert Stewart

Stewart was born in 1917 to John and Bessie Hilderly on the family farm near Innerkip. Some time after his father opened the Plattsville Chick Hatchery and the family moved to Plattsville. After finishing school Stewart worked in the Chick Hatchery. In 1941 he joined the army and took training in Camp Borden, Niagara Falls, Pennsylvania, Debert and St. John, New Brunswick. Until the end of the war he served with the Scots Fusiliers in Labrador. Stewart received his honourable discharge in late 1945.

Stewart worked in agriculture and at the Chick Hatchery, finally going with Canada Sand. In 1973 he married Margaret Miller of Shakespeare. He retired in 1978.

Stewart died on January 5th 1987.

KAUFMAN Harry Lindsay Serv.# 3136524

Harry was born on March 23rd 1896 to Albert and Elizabeth Kaufman on the home farm. After finishing school he worked with his father on the home farm. In 1915 he went out to Smiley, Saskatchewan on the harvest excursion. He joined the army on May 23rd 1918. He was 5 feet 8 1/2 inches tall with a chest girth, fully expanded, of 40 1/2 inches. His range of expansion was 3 inches. Harry was of fair complexion with blue eyes and brown hair. He had a congenital deformity of his left little finger.

On his honourable discharge in 1919 he took up agricultural work on the home farm and also went out to Smiley for harvests.

When the depression hit in 1930 Harry decided to settle in the west. He rode the rods on the freight trains to Saskatchewan. In due course he bought a farm and settled near Smiley in western Saskatchewan. In 1933 Harry came home and took Elizabeth Calder from Plattsville out to Smiley where they were wed.

On September 26th 1937 a son, Donald Calder was born. Perry Gordon followed on December 7th 1938. He was tragically killed in an automobile accident on August 17th 1968. Harry gradually expanded his farm until it consisted of 22 sections (a section is 640 acres). Harry did dry land farming with some irrigation and a fairly substantial cattle ranch.

The farm is now owned and run by his son, Donald who has expanded the farm to 27 sections, which is 17,280 acres. He has eschewed cattle and crops every acre.

Harry died in 1972.

KENNEDY Osmund McCallum

Mac was born on February 14th 1913 to Lorne and Jessie Kennedy at Bruce, Alberta 60 miles east of Edmonton. When Mac was three years old the family moved to Edmonton. In 1927 his father died and so the mother moved Mac and his sister Merle to Stratford where they both attended Normal School after finishing secondary school. Mac taught at Wellesley and Lambeth before joining the school in Plattsville. He taught for a few years in Plattsville and then joined the Royal Canadian Air Force (R.C.A.F.) during the Second World War. He served for four years and then went back to teaching at Hespeler, Ontario. He took the position of Town Clerk. In 1956 Mac was appointed as Clerk Treasurer at Deep River, Ontario. He was also an executive of the Ontario Municipal Association.

He married Beatrice Dukes on December 1st 1945. Beatrice had a daughter, Susan, from a previous marriage, so Mac adopted her as his own. They then had two sons, Brian was born on January 13th 1951 and Bruce on July 22nd 1952.

Mac died of a massive stroke on June 17th 1965.

KIRKLAND Stephen Merritt

Stephen was born on October 12th 1896 in Bright. After finishing school he worked in agriculture. On September 29th 1915 Stephen joined the army in Drumbo. His next of kin was his mother, Mrs. W.J. Ramsey. Steve was 5 feet 4 inches tall with a chest girth of 35 inches and 2 1/2 inches of expansion. He had blue eyes and brown hair with a fair complexion. Stephen was a Methodist and his picture is hung in the Bright United Church with all the other members of that church who were killed in the war.

Stephen was killed on June 8th 1916.

LAMBERT Maurice Albert

Maurice was born on September 9th 1913 in Woodstock to George Henry and Clara Lambert. He graduated from High School in 1931. The depression was in full swing and a man had to take whatever he could get. Maurice had several different jobs before enlisting in the Royal Canadian Air Force (R.C.A.F.) in April 1940. He took his training in Air Crew as an Observer. The Observers did the navigating and dropping the bombs or depth charges. On his graduation he was sent to Coastal Command on the East Coast flying Catalinas. It was their job to protect the convoys going to England from attacks by the German submarines. They escorted the convoys to the mid-Atlantic then escorted the ships coming back from England to Halifax. He was then posted to England and protected convoys from England to the Mid-Atlantic and back. On May 13th 1943 Maurice married Kathleen A. Wortley of Winnipeg. He received his honourable discharge in January of 1945.

He worked for the Dominion Government in the Veterans' Department until 1946 when he purchased a poultry farm near Bright through the Veteran's Land Act. He and Kae also started their family at this time. Leslie Bond was born on February 18th 1946. Daniel Maurice followed on October 26th 1947 then came Roderick George Henry on March 15th 1949. Nancy Evelyn completed the family on November 1st 1954.

Maurice and Kae operated a hatchery and developed their own breed of layers - "The Bright Cross". Maurice also wrote the poultry column for the Family Herald and the Canadian Poultry Review for many years.

In 1969 he was appointed Director of the North Blenheim Mutual Insurance. In 1973 he was appointed Manager, succeeding W.S. Hastings. In 1974 he sold the farm and built their new home on the Old School lot at the south end of Bright. Maurice retired in 1981.

Maurice died in May 1996.

LEONARD Lorne James

Plattsville Memorial Gates

Lorne was born on July 4th, 1916 to Charles and Zella (nee-Brown) Leonard. They lived on the Brown Farm across from the Chesterfield Church. Charles was a mailman. He was a victim of the flu epidemic and died in 1918. Zella moved to Bright and was employed as a school teacher at the Bright school. Lorne went to elementary school in Bright and then high school in the Plattsville Continuation School. He worked in agriculture until the war and then joined the Royal Canadian Air Force (R.C.A.F.). He was trained as a radio and radar mechanic. He was posted to Coastal Command in Newfoundland who used their radar to protect convoys from the German U-Boats.

In November of 1944 Lorne married Myrtle Irene Hogg. He received his honourable discharge in late 1945. They settled in Toronto where Lorne got a job with Rogers Majestic as his air force training and work fitted him perfectly for their need for employees with radio and radar knowledge. After a few years Phillips took over Rogers Majestic.

Donalda Charley was born on October 11th 1947. Joyce Grace completed the family on December 13th 1950. Lorne retired in 1972.

Lorne died in May 1975.

LINTON John George Hall Serv.# 2365888

Plattsville Memorial Gates

Hall was born to John and Elizabeth Linton on October 28th 1898 in Bright. Hall joined the army on July 23rd 1918 having been in the Canadian Officers Training Corps at the University of Toronto. On enlistment Hall was 19 years old. His height was 5 feet 8 inches and his chest fully expanded was 35 inches with a range of expansion of 5 inches. He had a fair complexion with blue eyes and brown hair.

LYLE Walter Frederick   Serv. # 157625

Washington Plaque

Walter was born on April 4th 1893 to Ethel Lucy Lyle in Middlesex County. After finishing school Walter was employed as a farm labourer. He joined the 81st Battalion on September 10th 1915. He was 5 feet 4 1/2 inches tall with a a chest girth of 36 1/2 inches fully expanded. His range of expansion was 3 1/2 inches. He had a fair complexion with blue eyes and light brown hair.

Walter was a member of the Church of England. He was transferred to the 4th Canadian Mounted Rifles of the Canadian Expeditionary Force. He died on January 25th, 1918 and is buried in the Toronto Prospect Cemetery, grave C #1691. Walter was a member of the Washington Church and his name is inscribed on a plaque in the church.

MacFARLANE James

James was born on March 19th 1918 to George Ross and Lavina (nee-Capling) MacFarlane in Plattsville. After finishing school Jim worked in agriculture. In late 1942 he joined the Royal Canadian Engineers. He was stationed in Winnipeg, Manitoba; Debert, Nova Scotia and Barriefield, Ontario.

He received his honourable discharge in the beginning of 1946. He bought a small farm of 50 acres just north of Plattsville, down the river road. He practised mixed farming and in 1949 he bought a truck and combined farming and trucking steel. Jim married Audrey Bowman from Pine Hill in 1960, unfortunately they had no children. Shortly after he got a job at Canada Sand, of course Audrey helped with the farm. Jim was very practical and had a great sense of humour, this made him many friends. He retired in the early 1980's.

Jim died on November 16th 1996.

MACKENZIE George Osborne

George attended Woodstock Collegiate Institute. His father, G. Mackenzie, was a farmer in West Zorra Township. George took up teaching as a vocation and taught at the Bright School where he was very highly thought of. He joined the Masonic Lodge in Plattsville and after he went overseas he wrote to the Lodge several times. While still in England George transferred to the Royal Flying Corps (R.F.C.) and became a fighter pilot. He was a pilot on the 56th Squadron of the R.F.C. George was killed in aerial combat near Arras on September 27th 1918. His name is on the Cenotaphs at Embro and at Chesterfield.

MARTIN McK.

Plattsville Memorial Gates

I can find no record of Mr. Martin other than the fact he graduated from the Plattsville Continuation School and joined the forces in World War II.

There was a Dr. Martin who was a vet in Bright but I am unable to find a trace of him either.

McDONALD Walter Glasgow

Walter was born on October 25th 1918 to Franklin Glasgow and Irene (nee-Oberer) McDonald and baptised on June 13th 1919. After finishing school Walter worked in agriculture, mainly on the home farm. On May 27th 1937 Walter married Ella Bond. Edythe Elizabeth, the first of six children, was born on May 31st 1938.

Walter enlisted in the army on April 6th 1942 in Woodstock and was sent to London for basic training. He was then posted to Prince George, British Columbia with the Oxford Rifles. His next stint was served in Wainwright, Alberta and then he was posted back to London. On December 29th 1944 Walter was discharged for medical reasons. He went back home to take up the family farm.

On May 12th 1944 John Alexander was born followed by Eleanor Carol on September 12th 1947. Kenneth Walter followed on December 7th 1948. Marilyn Ruth made her debut on April 14th 1952 and Sharon Marie completed the family on April 14th 1956.

Walter farmed and sold gravel out of a pit on the farm. In 1955 he started as a mail carrier and kept at it till 1991. Walter also became very active in the Royal Canadian Legion and the Independent Order of Foresters. He served as Zone Commander of the Legion from 1975 to 1977. He also served as High Chief Ranger in the Independent Order of Foresters for seven years. He organized and participated in the Remembrance Day services in Plattsville, Chesterfield, Tavistock and Sevastopol for many years.

Walter died on February 19th 1995.

McDONALD Wallace Alexander Serv.# 756001

Wallace was born on March 12th 1895 to Mrs. Susan McDonald in Plattsville. After finishing school he apprenticed in the trade of Tire Finisher and obtained employment in Kitchener. On November 2nd 1917 Wallace joined the Canadian Expeditionary Force (C.E.F.). He was 5 feet 6 3/4 inches tall with a chest girth when fully expanded of 36 1/2 inches and a range of expansion of 2 inches. He had a fair complexion with blue eyes and light brown hair. Wallace was a Baptist.

This picture was taken with a group of Plattsville Veterans on August 11th 1919.

McKENZIE J.

Plattsville Memorial Gates

I can find no record of Mr. McKenzie other than the fact he graduated from the Plattsville Continuation School and joined the forces in World War II.

Stewart Scott McKie is second from the left.

McKIE Stewart Scott   Serv. # R68176

Stewart was born on September 11th 1903. After finishing school he worked at the McKie Buggy Company, owned by his father, until it closed in 1925. He then went to work for Sam McLaughlin in Oshawa, a friend of his father who was also in the buggy business but Sam had branched out into the automobile business and was producing the McLaughlin Buick car. On August 11th 1928 Stewart married Mary Francis Railton. After working for Sam, Stewart went to work at the Simpson Department store in Toronto.

He and Mary had three children. Robert Railton was born on February 24th 1931, James Stewart on March 6th 1934 and Mary Margaret on August 23rd 1935. After he left Simpson's he bought Hall's Garage in Plattsville and stayed with that until he joined the Air Force in late 1940. He served 4 1/2 years in the Royal Canadian Air Force (R.C.A.F.) and worked his way up from Aircraftsman to Flying Officer. Stewart was stationed in Toronto, Trenton, London, Mountain View, Lachine, Domaine D'Estrelle and finally Jarvis for the last two years. He was an armaments instructor at Mountain View where they flew Fairey Battles, a single engine fighter with a twin machine gun in the rear seat. Stewart was up testing the guns and neglected to put on his safety belt. The pilot did an unexpected barrel roll and Stewart fell out of the plane. He managed to grab the guns on his way out and braced his feet on the fuselage until the pilot righted the plane, Stewart then fell back in. While in Jarvis the station ran out of practise bombs. Stewart was able to make enough to tide them over until a new shipment came in. He was honourably discharged in September of 1945.

After the war Stewart went to work at Canada Sand as Lab Director then was promoted to Director of Quality Control. He also started his own woodworking business in Plattsville. In the 50's he went with Electrohome, leaving them to buy an ice cream making business in Sutton. He sold this business and was hired as an accountant at Slessor's Pontiac Buick dealership in Newmarket. He retired in 1963 due to ill health.

Stewart died on November 17th 1966.

McKIE Frank Serv. # 406889

Frank McKie (Signaller) killed Sept 27th 1918

Frank's name is inscribed on the Cenotaphs in both Dicksons' Corners and Chesterfield. He was a Signaller in the First Light Trench Mortar Battery of the Canadian Field Artillery (C.E.F.). His mother was Belle Black.

Frank was killed in action on September 27th 1918. He is buried in the Ontario Cemetery at Sains-Les-Marquion Fr 481.

He was a member of the Bright Church and this picture is hung in the Church as a memorial.

McLAREN William Broughton

Bill was born on February 21st 1923 to Hugh and Lottie McLaren. His father died when he was very young so he lived with his grandparents Mr. and Mrs William Gracey at R.R. #1 Bright, Ontario. He took his Elementary School in Bright, and his High School at Plattsville Continuation School. He worked in agriculture for a short time and then got a job working on radios and instruments.

In December of 1942 Bill joined the Royal Canadian Air Force (R.C.A.F.) and was stationed in Toronto. He married Ruth Jackson on August 28th 1943. He took courses in instruments and then trained in radar. He was transferred to Regina for a few months, then back to Toronto. He received his honourable discharge in September 1945.

Bill and Ruth started their family with a daughter Donna born on January 25th 1945. Hugh then joined the family on May 31st 1952 and Brian completed the family on March 26th 1956.

When Bill got his discharge he and Ruth stayed in Toronto where Bill got a job with Taylor Safeworks. His experience with instruments in the Air Force was valuable to him. He started doing spray painting with Taylor and became a professional spray painter. He moved the family to Norwood near Peterborough and set up his own business doing spray painting.

Bill died suddenly at work on May 7th 1964.

McLENNAN Harold Douglas

Doug was born on November 30th 1914 to Dr. Donald and Katherine McLennan. After leaving school Doug worked in carpentry. He joined the army in the fall of 1939, shortly after war was declared. He joined the Royal Canadian Regiment and became a sergeant in their Support Company for a little better than five years. Douglas went overseas in May 1940 and was in England for about three years. He took part in the invasion of Sicily with his Regiment and then the invasion of Italy. He was wounded and sent to a hospital in North Africa. After his recovery he was sent back into action at the Marne River in Italy. The Canadians then fought their way North and successfully attacked the Hitler Line. His regiment was then sent to Belgium and Holland. He arrived home in September 1945 and received his honourable discharge.

Doug took up carpentry on his return, then in 1950 became an embalmer. Shortly after he obtained a position with Canada Customs in Woodstock. Doug retired from Canada Customs in 1975.

Doug died on December 27th 1992.

McLENNAN Mary Donalda

Mary was born on September 7th 1921 to Dr. Donald and Katherine McLennan in Plattsville. After she finished school Mary worked for the Sanatorium at Freeport. In December 1943 Mary joined the Canadian Women's Army Corps. She took basic training in Kitchener, then to Halifax for 15 months where she became an Ambulance Driver in the No. 1 Canadian Ambulance Corps. Mary was posted to England in January 1944 where she drove for the Headquarters of the Canadian Reinforcement Unit. She was then transferred back to the No. 1 Canadian Ambulance Corps as an ambulance driver. Mary came home on the Queen Elizabeth in December of 1945. The Queen Elizabeth was the largest ship afloat. Shortly after Mary received her honourable discharge.

Mary married Leland Leslie Stairs from Nakawick, New Brunswick in August of 1946. They lived in Gagetown till 1950, when they moved to Kitchener. Douglas Neil was born on March 25th 1947. Donna Lynn was born on October 16th 1950 and Linda Mae completed the family on October 1st 1954. Leland died on August 13th 1989.

Mary lives in Kitchener with her daughter Linda as of August 2002.

MIDDLETON Frederick Donald

Don was born on December 17th 1916 to Frederick and Nellie Middleton in Hamiota, Manitoba. After finishing school in 1934 Don was hired by the Royal Bank of Canada in Brandon, Manitoba. In 1937 he left the Bank and worked his way over to England on a coal freighter to join the Royal Air Force (R.A.F.). He was trained as a pilot and was posted to #5 R.A.F. bomber squadron flying Hampden bombers.

On April 8th 1939 Don married Ada Margaret Violet Roma Smith. On February 20th 1940 they had a son Robert Neil. On April 12th 1940 Don was shot down over Kristiansund in Norway, just seven weeks after the birth of his son. The squadron was bombing German naval units in the fjords around Kristiansund. Roma brought their son to Canada in October 1940. Don was a prisoner in Oflag 1VC till the spring of 1942 when he was transferred to Luft 111, a new camp for airmen. Don participated in escape attempts and was sent to Colditz as punishment. Shortly before the invasion of France, Don was repatriated to England for medical reasons (a very rare event) on the Gripsholme, a Swedish ship. Don had two brothers, one had been killed in a bombing raid on Germany, and Bruce, an older brother, was on #164 Transport Squadron stationed in Montreal. The C.O. let Bruce use his plane to fly to London, England. He picked Don up and brought him to Montreal, where his wife and son were living.

Don, after a much needed leave, was posted to North Brandon, Manitoba for a refresher course and he then was posted to St. Hubert in Quebec. Don received his honourable discharge in September 1945 and took a course in Chiropractic. After completion he set up his practice in Toronto.

In 1946 Don and Roma adopted Valerie Hope. He sold the practice in Toronto after three years and they went to England for six weeks. On their return Don set up a new practice in Sarnia. In the early 50's Don was hired by Ayerst Laboratories as a detail man.

In 1969 Don and Roma bought a house in Washington. Don retired in the late 70's and he and Roma were very active in making pottery.

Don died in October of 1990.

MILBURN Harold Wesley   Serv. # 3131119

Harold was born on July 20th 1895 to Albert Milburn at Bright, Ontario. After leaving school Harold apprenticed as a printer. He was working in Swift Current, Saskatchewan when he joined up on September 11th, 1917. Harold was posted overseas quite soon after.

He was a private in the 75th Battalion of the Canadian Expeditionary Force (C.E.F.) when he was killed on September 27th 1918 at 23 years of age. Harold is buried in the Cantimpre Canadian Cemetery at Sailly, France #148.

His name is inscribed on the Cenotaph in Chesterfield and his picture is hung in his church in Bright, the former Methodist Church that is now the United Church.

MOON Arnold Alfred   Serv. # 3137270

Arnold was born on April 3rd 1896 to Alfred and Susanna Moon outside of Woodstock on the Second Concession of the 10th Line. After completing school he worked in agriculture on the home farm and at neighbours. Arnold joined the army in the First World War and served overseas. He was 6 feet 1 3/4 inches tall with a fair complexion, blue eyes and light brown hair.

He received his honourable discharge on September 22nd 1919. Arnold married his sweetheart, Florence Ann Dixon a year later on October 19th 1920. They had two daughters, Florence Pearl born on October 28th 1921 and Ellen Susanna born on November 29th 1929.

Arnold bought a farm on the Second Concession, 10th Line, just south of Bright from James Carr in 1922. It was a mixed farm and he used to sell milk to the Bright Cheese Factory.

In the 1940's many farmers in the area were going into tobacco growing. Arnold was not in favour of tobacco and always said he would never sell his farm to a tobacco farmer. A Mennonite by the name of Baer wanted to buy the farm in 1952. He had a big family, and as Arnold was not in top shape he decided to sell. He and his wife then moved to Woodstock where Arnold became a janitor at the Sentinel Review.

Arnold died on March 19th 1971.

MOON Florence Pearl

Pearl Moon was born on October 28th 1921 to Arnold and Florence Moon of Bright. She attended Plattsville Continuation School and Woodstock Collegiate. After completing her schooling she worked for F.W. Woolworth Co. in Toronto. In April 1941 Pearl left Woolworth Co. and enlisted in the Royal Canadian Air Force (R.C.A.F.), (W.D.). She was posted to Manning Depot in Toronto then to # 14 Service Flying Training School at Aylmer, Ontario where she took a course in Flight Control. Her next posting was to Eastern Air Command in Halifax where she worked on the plotting tables. Pearl was promoted to Corporal. On November 22nd 1944 Pearl married John Francis Sinnott who hailed from Windsor. John was in the Royal Canadian Navy. Pearl received her honourable discharge in January 1945.

After John was given his discharge they moved to Thunder Bay where John was employed as a Captain on a tug. A daughter, Judith Anne was born on November 5th 1949. The family was completed on May 7th 1951 with the birth of a son, Michael John.

Her husband, John, died on August 14th 1989. In 2003 Pearl lives in a retirement home in Thunder Bay.

MURRAY Clara Elizabeth

Clara was born on October 4th 1923 to Ward and Mary (nee-Dibble) Murray, on the home farm between Bright and Innerkip. After finishing school she got a job in Woodstock at York Knitting Mills. In February of 1943 she joined the Women's Royal Canadian Naval Service. She was posted to Galt for basic training. After intensive training in coding she worked in a Department of the Canadian and North Atlantic Area in Halifax coding and decoding messages. Clara met her future husband in Halifax and he was in the Navy on a minesweeper.

Clara received her honourable discharge in July of 1945.

On June 18th 1946 Clara married Robert Clark MacFadden, in the Chesterfield Church. Clark lived in Port Colborne and worked at Stedmans. He was transferred to Oliver, British Columbia in 1954 and they have lived there ever since. They had five children. Patricia Clare was the first and arrived on April 20th 1947. Roberta Lynn followed on May 25th 1948. Mary Jane joined the family on November 7th 1952 followed by Jo Anne Lee on May 22nd 1954. The only son, Robert Larry, was born on August 16th 1959 and completed the family.

Robert died on September 28 1996. Clara, in 2003, still lives in their home just outside of Oliver, British Columbia.

MURRAY James George

Jim was born on September 6th 1910 to Henry George and Mary Ann Murray in Plattsville. He was the youngest of five children and the only boy. When Jim finished school he went to Queen's University in Kingston for a couple of years, however funds ran out so Jim had to leave.

He came back to Plattsville and was employed by Canada Sand. He joined the army in October 1941. He was stationed at Kitchener, then at Ottawa and finally at Camp Borden. He first joined the Royal Canadian Army Medical Corps and was then transferred to the Armoured Corps until his honourable discharge on October 17th 1944.

As Jim had worked at Canada Sand before joining the army he returned there for the remainder of his working life. He lived on the family home on the north edge of town on the river. He also bought a house just west of town in 1965. Jim had a few good friends. He was a very superior piano player, but seldom played unless he had a few libations. He was also an unusually well read individual. His father was a school teacher.

Jim's mother, Mary Ann, died on December 18th 1954. Jim retired in 1980. He bought a house in Kitchener and lived there for the balance of his life.

Jim died on July 8th 1994 and is buried in the Ayr cemetery.

NELSON Gordon

Plattsville Memorial Gates

Gordon's mother was a widow who ran a small grocery store in Plattsville.

He had a sister named Evelyn. After the war the family left town and nobody has any idea where the brother and sister went.

NEWMAN Walter Serv.# 675124

Chesterfield Cenotaph

Irthlingborough Church Tower

Walter was born on July 30th 1892 to George and Elizabeth Ann Newman of 60 Addington Rd., Irthlingborough, Wellingborough, Northants, England. Walter was a farmer by occupation. He was a memeber of the Church of England.

Walter enlisted in the First Ballalion of the Western Ontario Regiment on February 5th 1916. The girth of Walter's chest when fully expanded was 34 inches, the range of expansion was 3 inches. Walter was 5 feet 9 inches tall with blue eyes, light brown hair and a medium complexion. Walter worked for Havelock Parker of Bright. After enlisting he received training in Canada and then in England. Walter was killed in action on the third of May 1917. Walter's name is inscribed on the Cenotaph in Chesterfield. He is buried in the Aubigny Communal Cemetery Extension, the Grave Reference is 11. F. 35.

NURSE Harold Grey

Grey was born on April 16th 1920 to Dr. Harold and Mrs. Nurse. He joined the army in early 1942. He enlisted for the Medical Corps but as there were no openings in this branch he was sent as a cook to the Oxford Rifles in Prince George, British Columbia. While on furlough Grey was married to Marion Elizabeth Pittock on October 24th 1942. An opening came up in the Medical Corps so Grey was posted to Kingston as an operation room assistant. During this time a son James Harold was born on August 9th 1944. Grey was later posted to London where he was promoted to Sergeant. He was made a Surgeons' Assistant at Crumlin Hospital near London, Ontario.

After his discharge Grey entered the Ontario Veterinary College, graduating in 1950. While in Veterinary school a daughter, Dorothy Marie, was born on June 28th 1949. Kathleen Elizabeth completed the family on June 17th 1950. He then worked with the Health of Animals Division in the Department of Agriculture. After better than two years with the Department of Agriculture, Grey and his brother Dr. Howard Nurse, purchased Moore Veterinary Hospital in Grosse Pointe, Michigan in 1953.

Grey died in October 1985.

NURSE Roy Douglas

Roy was born on June 29th 1925 to Dr. Harold and Mrs. Nurse. He joined the Royal Canadian Air Force (R.C.A.F.) in 1943 and received training in Toronto, London and Prince Edward Island where he graduated as an Air Gunner. He was then posted to Three Rivers, Quebec for Commando training and was posted to England in August of 1944. He joined a bomber crew and flew bombing missions over Germany until the war ended. He returned to Canada in February 1946.

Roy entered the University of Waterloo for one year and then decided to join the R.C.A.F. permanent force. He became a pilot and flew in Transport Command.

He was posted to Trenton Air Base as Commanding Officer and retired with the rank of Lieutenant Colonel in 1976. Following retirement he accepted a position as Head Check Pilot of Instrument Ratings for Transport Canada at Pearson International Airport. He retired from that responsibility in 1987.

Roy married Martha Ellen Johnston on February 27th 1954. They had one daughter, Mary Ellen, born on September 21st 1955. A son, David Roy was born on January 7th 1957.

David was tragically killed in a car accident in 1973.

Roy died in November 1999.

NURSE William Howard

Howard was born on December 21st 1921 to Dr. Harold and Mrs. Nurse. On enlisting in the Royal Canadian Air Force (R.C.A.F). he was posted to Manning Depot at Lachine, Quebec. Howard was then posted to Calgary where he graduated as a wireless operator. The next posting was to Paulson, Manitoba where he took gunnery and graduated as a Wireless Air Gunner. He took his operational training at Penfield Ridge. His next posting was to Dartmouth, Nova Scotia for duty on Coastal Command. He was promoted to Flying Officer at this time. The aircrew on Coastal Command were utilized to protect convoys from German submarines. They would fly halfway across the Atlantic Ocean and be airborne for 24 hours. He volunteered for the Pacific and was moved to Moncton, New Brunswick. Victory in Japan Day arrived and a short time later he received his honourable discharge.

After leaving the Air Force Howard entered Ontario Veterinary College with his brother Grey. They both graduated in 1950. Howard worked for a short time with the Health of Animals Division, Department of Agriculture. He and his brother Grey, purchased Moore Veterinary Hospital in Grosse Pointe, Michigan in 1953.

On May 17th 1950 Howard married Patricia Ann Corrigan. They had one son Richard Douglas who was born on December 1st 1953. Leslie Ann was then born on August 19th 1955, and Susan Elizabeth followed on August 25th 1958 to complete the family.

Howard retired in 1986 and his son, now Dr. Richard Nurse took over the Veterinary Hospital and the practice.

PARKER Roy Mann Serv # R-191752

Roy was born in Bright on September 23rd 1922 to Havelock and Martha (nee-Mann) Parker. After finishing school Roy worked on the family farm and other adjoining farms. He joined the Royal Canadian Air Force (R.C.A.F.) on October 16th 1942 and was posted to Manning Depot in Toronto.

After a stint of guard duty he was posted to Victoriaville in Quebec for Initial Training School and graduated at the end of March 1943. Roy then went to Elementary Flying Training School (E.F.T.S.) and graduated in July. At this time the Commonwealth Air Training Plan had graduated so many pilots that no more were needed so Roy was posted back to Toronto to remuster. He was sent to Bombing and Gunnery School in Mossbank, Saskatchewan. After two months of Bombing and Gunnery he was posted to St. Thomas for photography. Roy wasn't too passionately fond of this so remustered to General Duties. He went on fire picket for two months, then was posted to St. Hubert in Quebec for two months.

In late summer 1944 Roy was posted overseas and shipped out of Halifax on the Mauretania. He ran into Philip Grimes on the boat and hasn't seen him since. He was posted to London Headquarters in the Mail Department. His next posting was to Down Ampney where they flew supplies to our troops in Holland, and after the war ended, food parcels for the Dutch people. When that finished Roy was posted to Bournemouth and then shipped home in April 1946. Roy was discharged at the end of May 1946. He was awarded the Canadian Volunteer Service Medal (C.V.S.M.) and Clasp, The King George Medal and the War Service Medal.

He went home and found suitable employment at the New Dundee Creamery where he became a butter and cheese maker. Roy stayed with them until he retired.

On January 10th 1948 Roy married Geraldine AnnAdele Eckstein. They had four children. Bruce Arnold was born on April 21st 1948 followed by Dianne Marie on April 20th 1949. Elaine Louise was born on September 26th 1950 and Wendy Jane completed the family arriving on October 24th 1958.

Roy retired in 1987 and in 2003 still enjoys married life in New Dundee.

PARKER Willis Franklin

Willis was born on June 3rd 1914 to Havelock and Martha Parker of Bright. After finishing school he worked for two years for Ab Pearson and Frank Yeo of Innerkip.

In late 1941 he joined the Royal Canadian Air Force (R.C.A.F.) and took his Manning Depot in Toronto. He did Security Guard duty at various stations and then graduated to the Military Police. Willis went overseas as an M.P. in the late fall of 1944. He returned to Canada in the fall of 1945 and received his honourable discharge shortly after.

Willis returned to the farm and worked with his dad and on other adjoining farms in the area. In the late forties and early fifties he was driving transport for Lowes Transport. On January 23rd 1953 Willis married Margaret Jean Robertson. By this time he was working for Bigham The Mover out of Woodstock. They moved to Woodstock and raised their family there.

Willis and Margaret had four children, Kenneth Roy born on November 17th 1956, Kathryn Florence on January 30th 1958, then Robert William followed on March 21st 1959 and Cheryl Lynn completed the family on September 23rd 1963. Margaret died on October 24th 1977. Willis kept busy working part time for a local cartage company in Woodstock. He was an active member of his church and a volunteer in the community.

Willis died on May 10th 1993.

PARKHOUSE Francis William

Frank was born in England on December 17th 1903. He came to Canada as a Bernardo Boy in the early twenties from St. Albans Diocese. For a few years Frank worked on the Thibodeau farm west of Plattsville. In the fall of 1928 he went out to Saskatchewan on the harvest excursion. Many young men went west for the harvest as they could make very good money for up to three months. On April 15th 1931 he married Myrle Etta Thibodeau, the daughter of the man he worked for. They had two sons, Raymond William was born on September 16th 1934 and Lloyd Francis who was born on July 3rd 1941.

Frank joined the Oxford Rifles in 1941. He received training at Camp Borden and was then posted to Listowel on a commando course. He was promoted to Sergeant and posted to London for further training. In late 1942 and early 1943 he was stationed in Prince George and promoted to Sergeant. He then was posted to Nanaimo for further training and promoted to Sergeant-Major. His next postings were to Wainright, Alberta; Courtney, British Columbia; London and Ipperwash. He was honourably discharged in April 1946.

Frank settled down in Plattsville and worked at Canada Sand until he retired. He was very active in the community and served on the Plattsville School Board. He also served on the Waterloo Oxford School Board when the new Secondary School was built just outside of Baden. Frank was elected to the Blenheim Township Council for five years. He was also a member of the Masonic Lodge.

The eldest son died tragically on July 30th 1955. Frank died on May 22nd 1979, his wife Myrle passed away on March 6th 1987.

PATTERSON Howard Brock

Pat was born on June 22nd 1920 to William and Edna Patterson in Galt. They moved to Leamington where Pat took his schooling. At the end of the thirties Hitler took over Austria and then negotiated with Chamberlain for 'Peace in our Time' over Czechoslovakia. The ink was barely dry on the agreement when the Germans marched into the Sudetenland, a province of mainly German descent.

When war came in September 1939 twelve of the boys in Pat's class joined the Royal Canadian Air Force in aircrew. Only two came back.

Pat received his wing as an Air Observer on December 28th 1941. He left Halifax for England on February 28th 1942. Shortly after he was posted to England Pat wound up in Invergordon converting to Flying Boats.

His course was completed on August 29th 1942 and with a short leave met some old school buddies from Leamington. Pat and his crew then flew to Gibraltar and joined Coastal Command flying Catalinas out of Gibraltar. Their job was to fly over the Atlantic, and sometimes the Mediterranean, and help protect convoys of merchant ships from submarines. They were always out for at least 24 hours and Pat had to be on duty the whole time. Pat completed a tour and was sent home for furlough. He then returned to England and was posted to another Coastal Command squadron flying out of Northern Ireland on Sunderland Flying Boats. The Sunderland had four Pegasus motors, not the best motor in the world. Pat finished a tour on the Sunderlands. In due course he was posted home and received his discharge on May 3rd 1945.

Pat started in dentistry in September of 1945 at the University of Toronto. It was not his bag so at the end of 1946 he went to work for Bell Telephone. On May 19th 1947 Pat married Joan Dean Lendon. They had two daughters, the first Mary Carol Aleine was born on March 6th 1948. Barbara Joan followed on May 9th 1953.

Pat and Joan moved to Washington in June of 1972. Pat retired from Bell in the spring of 1981. He raised very superior vegetables and sold them on the road from a large table. Change was available in an open drawer. Pat said he was never ripped off by any customer or passer-by.

Joan developed emphysema and tragically died on October 16th 1993.

Pat died on January 27th 1996.

PEAT Norman Wallace

Norman was born on January 8th 1916 to James Wallace and Maggie (nee-Hogarth) Peat of Bright, Ontario.

Sentinel Review, Woodstock. L.A.C Norman W. Peat, son of Mr. Wallace Peat, Bright, enlisted last September (1940) and is in training with the Royal Canadian Air Force (R.C.A.F.) in Prince Albert, Saskatchewan L.A.C Peat was educated at Ratho Public School, Plattsville Continuation School, Woodstock Collegiate and Toronto Normal School. He took courses at Brandon, Winnipeg and Regina before being transferred to Prince Albert.

Sentinel Review, Woodstock. Out-gunned, out-paced, out numbered but never out fought W/O Norman Wallace Peat skilfully manouvered his Lysander to not only beat off the attack of two Focke-Wulf 190's but also to inflict damage on one of them. Peat's Lysander was pounced on by the two German fighters with their 4 cannons, two machine guns and top speed of 326 m.p.h. in contrast to the high-winged Lysander with four machine guns and no speed.

The 26 year old Peat, who joined the air force in September 1940, took his aircraft right down to the sea with no cloud cover. "The F.W.s came at us line abreast at first, and I did a complete circle to get out of the way. They then came back at us one from each side. I hardly knew how to get out of that fix, but I turned part of a circle and back again. They then made a third attack from astern. By this time I was doing violent 'S' turns. After the third attack the gunner-observer got in a long burst at one of the enemy as he turned away. The remaining F-W took another crack at them and left for home. The fight only lasted four or five minutes."

Letter to Miss J Hogarth 8th of November 1945 from Royal Canadian Air Force (R.C.A.F.) in Ottawa.
"I am directed to refer to your letter of 1st October, 1945, and to state that your nephew, Flying Officer N. Peat was the pilot of a walrus aircraft which set out to rescue a pilot in the sea, fifty three miles north of Bone, Algeria. A message from the aircraft stated that the rescue was successful but that one of the aircraft floats had been lost. An Air Sea Rescue Launch and Beaufighter were detailed to carry out a search, but unhappily no trace was found of the Walrus Aircraft or any of her crew. In these circumstances it is feared that no further news can be expected of your nephew. I am to add that 283 Squadron at the time your nephew was reported a casualty, was stationed in North Africa."

A large crowd of relatives gathered in the Presbyterian Church at Ratho on Sunday May 26th 1946 to honour the memory of F/O Norman W. Peat who was reported missing May 27th 1943 while serving with the Air Sea Rescue Squadron 283 B.N.A.F. Norman was 21 years old.

PERRY Lloyd Robertson   Serv. # 356218

Lloyd was born on October 17th 1911 in Deloraine, Manitoba, the son of George and Fanny Perry. He went to the University of Manitoba and enrolled in the Faculty of Engineering. While at University he joined the Canadian Officers Training Corps, but with the depression, money dried up so Lloyd had to get a job. As jobs were extremely scarce Lloyd had to turn his hand to anything he could get. Lloyd was related to the Thompson family so came to Plattsville and was employed by Canada Sand as a millwright.

Lloyd married Jean Catherine English on January 18th 1941. Shortly after, on July 29th 1941 he joined the Army Service Corps in London, Ontario and was placed with the Royal Canadian Electrical and Mechanical Engineers where he served for 4 years. He was sent to Brockville for three months and was promoted to 2nd Lieutenant. He was then posted to Camp Borden for four months and was promoted to 1st Lieutenant.

He was stationed in Ottawa for two months before being shipped overseas in April 1942. Shortly after being posted to England, Lloyd was promoted to Captain. He was in England until November 1944, then served in France, Belgium, Holland and Germany with the 4th Division. Lloyd arrived home on September 14th 1945 and received his honourable discharge on October 22nd 1945.

White Motor Company hired Lloyd on the 12th of November 1945 and after six months of training he was made a Supervisor. He remained in the trucking industry until 1960 when he joined the Alberta Gas Trunk Line (Nova Corp.) as a Supervisor. He retired in 1975. In his retirement he very much enjoyed gardening, fishing, camping and travelling.

Brian John, the first son of Jean and Lloyd, was born on May 24th 1947. A brother, Glen Francis, arrived on July 15th 1951. Lloyd then became very active in the Boy Scout movement.

Jean died on February 20th 1988. Lloyd later married Marguerite Swanson. In 1994, on the 50th Anniversary of D Day, Lloyd returned to the Normandy beaches to take part in the ceremonies.

Lloyd died on December 6th 1994.

POLL William Orville   Serv. # 1058426

Orville was born to Victor and Grace Poll on December 9th 1924. He was raised by his grandparents Adam and Annie Poll who farmed on Lot 5 on the 14th Concession of Blenheim Township. Orville attended the school at Perry's Corners. After finishing school he worked on the home farm until he joined the army in January 1943. He was posted to Camp Borden and trained as a Despatch Rider. In the army he was known as Bill. He was then posted to Debert in Nova Scotia for a short time before being shipped overseas in September 1943. He was appointed an instructor for Despatch Riders. Bill went into France on the D-Day attack with the Royal Canadian Armoured Service Corps. He was wounded at Caen in his leg, arm and back and was in a cast for eleven months.

He was posted back to Canada in 1945 and was sent to Westminster Hospital in London and then Christie Street Hospital in Toronto.

Bill received his honourable discharge in 1946 and moved to Kitchener. He then used the name Orville and obtained employment at J.M. Schneider.

In 1948 Orville married Mildred Kaminski who had a daughter Ruth Ann from a previous marriage, born in 1943. Orville adopted her as his own. Their first child, William Jr. was born on May 15th 1949. Mary Lou completed the family in 1953.

In 1964 Orville left Schneiders and bought a resort at Three Mile Lake near Bracebridge. He and Mildred ran the resort for 12 years when Orville sold it and retired to Skeleton Lake.

Orville died on April 8th 1988.

PRATT Thomas

Thomas Pratt was in the First World War. He married before the war and had a son who moved to the United States. This picture was taken on August 11th 1919. His first wife died and Tom married Jessie Fergusson of Plattsville in the early thirties.

RAILTON Samuel Victor

Victor was born in 1906 to Rev. Richard and Sarah Railton in Kelvin, Ontario. In the early 1920's Richard accepted a call to the Plattsville Methodist Church where Victor graduated from the Plattsville Continuation School and then enrolled in the University of Toronto Medical School graduating with his M.D. in 1929. He set up his practice in Port Colborne. In 1929 Victor also married Ruth Miriam Hazlewood.

They started a family with Richard Hazlewood born on November 8th 1931. Eleanor Jane arrived in February of 1933 followed by Nancy Miriam in 1938.

In 1939 Victor joined the Medical Corps with the rank of Captain. He was posted to the 2nd Light Field Ambulance unit in Camp Borden. The unit was then posted to Valcartier, Quebec and to England in 1940. He was transferred to #2 Canadian Field Hospital and then to the Forestry Corps in Scotland. He received his promotion to Major and was appointed Officer Commanding the #6 Field Surgical Unit. They went in with the invasion and up through France, Belgium and Holland.

Dr. Railton received his honourable discharge in late summer of 1945 and resumed his practice in Port Colborne. Ruth and Victor wanted one more son to balance the family and in 1946 got their wish with the birth of James Victor. Dr. Railton moved to Welland and was a Surgeon in the Hospital. He was soon appointed Chief of Staff. He was actively involved in the Liberal party and was elected M. P. for his riding and made a worthwhile contribution for seven years with Trudeau.

Dr. Railton retired in 1981 but remained active and committed. He died at 91 years of age in 1997.

RANCK Howard Frederick Serv. # A-82023

Howard was born on February 27th 1917 to Mr. and Mrs. Fred Ranck in Plattsville. As with most young people from Plattsville he went to work at Canada Sand after finishing school. He married Mildred Eileen Steinman on November 23rd 1940.

In early 1942 Howard joined the Oxford Rifles and was posted to Kitchener and London for training. In the late summer of 1942 the Regiment was posted to Prince George, British Columbia.

On October 2nd 1942 his son, Terrance Howard was born in St. Mary's Hospital in Kitchener. The bill for the stay at the hospital is reproduced below. On May 10th 1943 he was shipped overseas and posted to the Irish Regiment of Canada. Shortly after the unit was posted to North Africa and then Italy. On the 17th of April 1944 Howard received two bullet wounds, one in the neck and the other in the right shoulder. On October 24th 1944 a mine explosion ripped the tip of his nose and a piece of shrapnel lodged in his upper back. The unit was withdrawn at the end of the Italian campaign and sent to Belgium and Holland. He arrived home in December of 1945 and received his honourable discharge in January of 1946.

Howard went to work at the Post Office in Kitchener and in due course was transferred to the office in Preston. A daughter, Linda Joan, was born to Howard and Mildred on April 4th 1948.

Howard died on August 5th 1970.

I Accounts Must Be Paid Weekly In Advance

All Overdue Accounts Will Be Charged Interest at Current Rates

KITCHENER,.............Oct. 12, 1942...
ONTARIO

Mrs. Mildred Ranck...................................

.................Baden, Ontario........................

In Account With **ST. MARY'S HOSPITAL**

From Oct. 1-1942	To Oct. 12-1942			
Mother	2 day @ $2.35 per day	. . .	4	70
Babe	1 days .90 " "	. . .		90
Mother	9 days @ 3.00 " "		27	00
Operating Room Fee	Case Room		5	00
Special Nurse's Board				
Ex-Ray				
Lab.	Urinalysis		3	00
Extras	Medicine		1	80
			42	40
SMH	Phone call			10
			42	50

RELLINGER Raymond Kenneth

Kenneth was born on September 2nd 1925 to Norman and Meta Rellinger. The home farm was just north of Perry's Corners where Ken went to school. When he graduated from Elementary School he went to Plattsville for High School.

In November 1943 Ken joined the Royal Canadian Air Force (R.C.A.F.) and was sent to Manning Depot in Toronto. He had just started his Initial Training School (I.T.S.) when he was hospitalized for two hernia operations. He then completed I.T.S., but as there was a surplus of aircrew he went through a discharge to Aircrew Reserve. Ken joined the army and in 1945 took his basic training and then was posted to Ipperwash for advanced training. Shortly after Ken was hospitalized for a broken ankle and pneumonia. He then finished his advanced training and was given his honourable discharge in May 1946.

Ken went to Cambridge and was employed in the textile industry. After a few months he went with Franklin Manufacturing. In 1962 Kenneth married Ruth Doreen Drinkwater.

In 1983 Kenneth retired. He and Ruth are in good health and in 2003 enjoying their retirement in Preston.

RENNICK James Thomas   Serv.# B105262

James was born on September 27th 1926 on his parents farm near Bright. He attended the Bright Public School and the Plattsville Continuation School. James enlisted in the Royal Canadian Air Force (R.C.A.F.) at London, Ontario. He reported to #1 Manning Depot in Toronto on September 28th 1944. He was given Air Force Service # R289851.

After a short time the recruits were given the choice of a discharge or joining the army as many Royal Canadian Air Force (R.C.A.F.) air training stations were closing. James chose to join the army and was given a new service # B105262. He was sent to Newmarket, Ontario on October 24th 1944 for basic training. His draft completed this course on December the 15th and was then posted to Ipperwash, Ontario for advanced training which was completed on March 8th 1945. His unit was sent to Vernon, British Columbia and were stationed at Vernon and Chilliwack, British Columbia until Victory in Japan (V.J.) Day. The unit was returned to Toronto and James received his honourable discharge at No. 2 District Depot in Toronto on October 31st 1945.

Jim returned to his parents farm and stayed until 1947 when he moved to Kitchener. He married Marion Fenn, a teacher from Plattsville. He got into the construction business in Kitchener and in due course took a partner, Alf Brown by name. Business was good. They expanded and were soon also building houses in Stratford and Deep River.

Marion and Jim had five children. Mary Gail was born on June 19th 1949, Susan Margaret came on April 23rd 1951. Patricia Marion arrived on November 7th 1955. Thomas James was born on April 22nd 1961 and Jack Edward, the last of the children, was born on September 6th 1966.

Jack loved travelling and photography and while indulging both those passions in New Zealand was tragically killed in a fall on January 8th 1988.

Jim received his commercial pilots license in 1956 after the family moved to Deep River. He enjoyed flying fishermen into camps in Quebec. Marion and Jim enjoyed Air Shows and in 1951 began to attend them regularly. They attended many air shows in Canada, U.S.A. and even Farnborough in England.

Marion died at their home in Ottawa on August 31st 1998.

In 2003 Jim continues to lead an active life in Ottawa.

RENNICK John Stanley Serv. # R99592

Jack was born in the village of Bright to Stanley and Ada Rennick on May 23rd 1921. He attended the Bright Elementary School and went on to the Plattsville Continuation School. Jack drilled wells with his Dad and planned on resuming well drilling after the war.

His one big love was hockey which he played from an early age. He played defence in the local league and also in the Ontario Hockey Association (O.H.A.) in all three categories, Junior, Intermediate and Senior. In 1938-39 he played Intermediate for the Woodstock Devils and they were the O.H.A. Intermediate finalists. He always wore sweater # 3. He played for the Woodstock Trojans in 1939-40 and then for the London-Woodstock Combines (Sr. O.H.A.) in 1940-41. On January 4th 1941 they played an exhibition game against Kitchener and Jack scored the winning goal in overtime. Old timers will remember Howie Meeker, a New Hamburg lad who played for Kitchener at that time. Jack was scouted by the Detroit Red Wings, but he joined the Royal Canadian Air Force (R.C.A.F.) on April 16th 1941 at London, Ontario.

He was posted to Manning Depot in Toronto and from there to several stations for air crew training. He graduated as an Air Gunner and was sent overseas from Halifax on October 26th 1942. His group arrived in England on November 4th 1942. They must have gone over on the Queen Elizabeth or the Queen Mary . The Q.E. and Q.M. went alone and only took a week. After further training at an Operational Training Unit and Conversion Unit he was posted to #12 Squadron, a Royal Air Force (R.A.F.) Bomber Squadron at Wickenby in Lincolnshire on April 25th 1943. Along the way Jack became engaged to a young Womens Auxilliary Air Force (W.A.A.F), by the name of Doreen Worsley. The Squadron flew Lancasters and Jack was a Flight Sergeant Air Gunner. They had a few operations over Germany. On June 25th 1943 on a test flight the port outer wing broke off and the plane crashed near Stenigott in Lincolnshire killing all the crew.

Jack is buried in the Cambridge City Cemetery, England in grave #14534 alongside another Canadian crew member, Paul Soluk.

Jack was always a happy and fun loving man. He is still missed.

RENNICK Stanley   Serv. #348243

Stan was born on November 23rd 1895 in the stone cottage one mile west of Ratho. He was the eldest son of Thomas and Mary Rennick and spent his youth on his father's farm on the 12th Concession of Blandford Township. Stan went to Ratho School and then to Business College. He graduated from Stratford Business College on June 13th 1913. The building later served as a bank. He worked in Toronto as a bookkeeper until he enlisted in the army.

Stanley enlisted at Kingston, Ontario on June 28th 1915 in the Royal Canadian Horse Artillery. On October 3rd 1915 he was posted to the Canadian Expeditionary Force and went overseas on the S.S. Missanoli. He arrived at Shorncliffe Military Camp in England on December 28th 1915. He spent 10 months in France with the Canadian Field Artillery as a driver and gunner. Stan was gassed in a German gas attack.

On August 23rd 1918 Stan was posted to the 16th Brigade Canadian Field Artillery as a driver and gunner. This brigade left Scotland for Archangel in Russia on September 21st 1918 on H.M.S. Stephen and arrived on September 30th. He spent nine months in Russia helping the White Russians against the Reds (Communists). The Reds prevailed so the Brigade returned to Scotland on the H.M.C.S. Czarita on June 11th 1919. While in England Stanley met and married Ada M. Sturdey in Folkstone on October 17th 1917. Her parents were James and Mary Sturdey from Woodchurch, Kent and Ada was born on February 26th 1896. Stan, the Canadian Brigade members and their families sailed from Southampton on the "Adriatic" arriving in Halifax at 8:00 P.M. on September 10th 1919. He received his honourable discharge in Halifax and was awarded the British War Medal and the Victory Medal.

Stanley and Ada had six daughters and two sons. Hazel Irene was born on March 31st 1918, James Thomas was born on May 20th 1920 and died 10 days after birth, John Stanley arrived on May 23rd 1921. He was killed on June 25th 1943 in the R.C.A.F. on Bomber Command. Mary Elizabeth was born on April 29th 1923. Laura Jean joined the family on October 6th, 1925 and Edna Mae followed on September 6th 1926. Marjory Joan was born on November 3rd, 1931 and Eva Joyce completed the family on April 2nd, 1933.

In 1921 Stan started drilling wells and did so for over 33 years. In 1922 he bought the house on James Street in Bright and both Ada and he spent the rest of their lives in that house. For a while he also had a coal business.

Stan belonged to the Woodstock Fish and Game Club. He was also Secretary Treasurer of the Plattsville Legion for a number of years. He belonged to the Plattsville Masonic Lodge and was fairly active in politics. He played the violin, had a good sense of humour and was an honest man.

Stanley died on January 15th 1954.

RENNICK Thomas Serv. # 2010193

Thomas was born on May 13th 1898 to Thomas and Mary Rennick in the stone cottage one mile west of Ratho. In early 1918 he tried to enlist in the Air Force and was told they had a surplus of recruits so on May 15th 1918 he enlisted in the army with the Royal Canadian Engineers. He was trained as a sapper at St. John, New Brunswick until June 12th and was then posted to Amherst, Nova Scotia. From Amherst they were sent to Halifax and boarded the H.M.S. Huntsend and sailed for England. They arrived at Birkenhead on August the 15th and immediately commenced training at Bouley Camp, Aldershot. Tom contracted Scarlet Fever and was sent to Connaught Hospital. While in the hospital he was visited by his brother Stanley and John Shearer who were back from France. Tom then trained at Seaforth from October 4th until

November 11th 1918. Tom went to Ireland on leave and was a bit late in returning. Fortunately the ship was ready to leave for Canada so he was told to grab his kit and get on board.

After his discharge from the army he worked as a cowboy on a ranch in Alberta. In the fullness of time he met Annie Sylvester from Carmen, Manitoba. They were married on April 8th 1925. They took over Tom's parents farm near Ratho until 1953 when they sold it and retired to Woodstock, Ontario. During the time they were on the farm Tom served as President of the Bright Branch of the Royal Canadian Legion. He was also a member of the local School Board and active with the Bright Cheese Factory.

After moving to Woodstock they travelled by car to California, Las Vegas and back. Tom had his first flight in 1919 and Annie her first in 1930. They flew to England and Ireland in 1966 and toured the ancestral area near Ballymena in Ireland. Tom and Annie had two sons. James Thomas was born on September 27th 1926. William Edward was born on September 20th 1931.

Annie passed away on June 26th 1974 and Tom made annual visits to her Manitoba home for many years. Tom died on January 24th 1992.

RHODENIZER Ernest Everett

Ernie was born on June 15th 1911 in Lunenberg County in Nova Scotia to Calder and Eva Rhodenizer. He attended Bridgewater High School and was a runner in track and field. He played goal in hockey and pitched in baseball for Bridgewater teams. After he finished his schooling in 1929 he worked on farms and on ships.

In the early 1930's Ernie moved to Ontario and got a job with Firestone Tires in Hamilton. In the mid-thirties Ernie moved to Plattsville and worked on Roy Main's farm. He also pitched ball in a semi-pro league.

On September 2nd 1939 Ernie married Lloy Pratt in Plattsville. Lloy was the daughter of Alex and Julia Pratt who owned and operated the Temperance House in Plattsville. Lloy and Ernie had one child, Owen Ernest, born in Plattsville on November 30th 1940. Ernie worked at Canada Sand for a time and then in 1942 he joined The Royal Canadian Navy. He served at H.M.C.S. Provost in London for two months, from Provost he was posted to H.M.C.S. Cornwallis in Nova Scotia for nine months training then to Shelburne for a further seven months. He was then drafted to the Corvette 'Left Bridge' and served as a stoker till the end of the war. Ernie received his honourable discharge on June 4th 1945.

Ernie went back to working at Canada Sand. After a fair stint he decided to go into business for himself selling General Insurance. In January 1962 the three schools of Plattsville, Blinkbonnie and Washington were consolidated into a new school building in Plattsville. Ernie was engaged as a full time custodian. The staff relied on Ernie to keep the school spotless and the electrical and mechanical equipment functioning at all times. Ernie never disappointed them. The students adored him, as he took an interest in them all. He retired in June of 1976.

Ernie died on March 4th 1986. He is buried in the Plattsville Cemetery.

RICHMOND Elizabeth Young

Elizabeth was born on March 13th 1879 to James and Barbara Richmond at their home near Washington. She received her nurses training in New York City. Shortly after the First World War started Elizabeth joined the nursing corps and was sent overseas.

The photograph in her nurse's uniform was taken in Liverpool, England.

When the war ended she came home and in 1919 returned to New York for private nursing. In 1935 she retired to Galt to live with her mother and later her sister at 15 Blenheim Rd. While living there she did some nursing duties with the firm of Goldie McCullough .

Elizabeth died on January 24th 1956 in her 77th year. She was buried in the family plot in the Ayr cemetery.

Wedding picture of Harry Tew and Mary Richmond on September 1st 1909. Bestman George Oliver, Bridesmaid is Mary's sister Elizabeth Richmond

Medal from King George V

RITCHIE Alexander William Gratton

Alex was born on June 17th 1918. He joined the Territorial Army (equivalent to our militia) on November 20th 1935 with the Argyle and Sutherland Highlanders.

The Argyles were mobilized on September 2nd 1939 and sent to France in late December 1939. The Argyles were a mobile machine gun battalion. They were stationed at first in Armentieres until the end of January when they were positioned in the Maginot Line. The Germans attacked on the 12th of May in 1940. The Argyles being a mobile machine gun battalion were moved into Belgium. They dug in during daylight and moved back at night, always giving covering fire to our infantry. The Germans had overwhelming armoured superiority but our troops were able to slow their advance. Soon our troops were pinned against the Straits of Dover at Dunkirk. The British Government called in every boat, both civilian and military, to assist in the evacuation of our army. The Argyles were in the rearguard and out of the 48 men in Alex's platoon, 28 were killed. The rest, along with Alex, were taken prisoner on June 5th 1940. They were marched through Belgium and Holland to Germany for over two weeks. In Germany they were loaded on cattle cars. The sides of the cars had painted on them "40 men or 8 horses" in French. It wasn't luxurious, but it beat marching and they were happy to have the transportation. Several days later they arrived at Stalag V111B just outside of Lamsdorf. Alex was shipped to Oflag XX1B at Scubin and later to Stalag Luft 111 at Sagan, roughly 90 miles southeast of Berlin. The successful Wooden Horse escape was from this camp and all three participants got back to England. The Great Escape also happened here, and fifty of the escapees were shot after recapture.

The beginning of January 1945 the Russians got too close so the Germans marched the prisoners out to the west. It was colder than charity and the men were carrying everything they owned on their backs. It was very difficult. In March they finished at a camp near the town of Badorb. On Easter Sunday the Americans liberated them. Alex was demobilized in February 1946 and returned home. He went into construction for some time then became a Civil Defence Officer.

On February 14th 1947 Alex married Elizabeth Cummings Maize. They had three children. Graham Richard was born on November 13th 1947 and Elspeth Cummings Maize followed on August 16th 1951. Neil Alexander completed the family on December 1st 1955. In 1980 Alex retired and he and Elizabeth moved to Plattsville to be near their daughter Elspeth who had married Walter Molloy. Alex became active in the church and the Legion. He has always been involved with the November 11th Remembrance day services and for the past few years has organized and run them.

Elizabeth died on November 28th 1996.

In 2004 Alex still resides in Plattsville.

RITCHIE Elizabeth Cummings (nee-Maize)

Betty was born on November 17th 1924 in Hamilton, Scotland to Richard and Elizabeth Maize. She took her schooling at St. Johns Grammar School in Hamilton graduating in 1941. She then went into training as a nurse at Motherwell General Hospital. After completing her training, she joined the National Nursing Reserve and in 1942 was posted to Kilearn Military Hospital at Loch Lomond. This hospital dealt mainly with head and spinal injuries. It was here that Betty met Alex who was stationed at Montrose Castle on the bonny, bonny banks of Loch Lomond.

Romance blossomed and on February 14th 1947 Alex and Betty were wed. The three children they had are noted on the facing page under Alex' name. They now have seven grandchildren, three in England, three in Canada, and one in Italy.

Betty returned to nursing in 1954, retiring in 1980 when Alex also retired. They then moved to Plattsville to be near their daughter Elspeth.

Betty died on November 28th 1996.

RITTER Archibald Carl

Carl was born to John and Maria Magdelena (nee-Eix) Ritter on April 18th 1906 on the home farm west of Elmira. At age 17 he went to Toronto Teachers College and started teaching in one room schools as soon as he finished college. He then, while teaching, completed a B.A. at Queens by attending summer school and taking winter correspondence courses. He then attended the University for his fourth year to get his Honours Degree in Math and Physics. He furthered his knowledge at the University of Toronto with a Bachelor of Pedagogy. Carl then taught at the Plattsville Continuation School (we now call them Secondary Schools) and after a few years was appointed Principal of Leamington Secondary School. He married Ann Milne and they started a family with Jessie Marie, born on December 1st 1938. Archibald Robert Milne followed on October 29th 1941. Douglas James Donald completed the family on February 18th 1947.

Carl joined the Royal Canadian Air Force (R.C.A.F.) in the summer of 1941. He was posted overseas and was involved in setting up training schools for Canadian service men. After his honorable discharge he was a Public School Inspector in the Sudbury area. Many of the schools could be reached only by freight train (so he rode the caboose) and two only by canoe. In 1950 he was hired as Director of Education in Kingston and led a five member teacher education team in Kenya for five years to help them strengthen teacher training and so improve their education system. Mr. Ritter returned to Kingston in 1973 to retire and Queen's University gave him a well deserved honorary LLD degree. He stayed involved in education to the end, promoting and assisting in the writing of school histories for all the schools in Kingston and Frontenac County.

Carl died on October 2nd 1989 at Kingston General Hospital.

RONALD James Edwin

Edwin was born to James and Christa-Ann Ronald in 1896.

After finishing school he worked in agriculture on the home and neighbouring farms. He joined up early in the war and served with the Canadian Divisional Signal Corps. He was gassed at Ypres and when he returned to Canada was sent to the Freeport Sanatorium in Kitchener.

Edwin died at the Sanatorium on July 11th 1923 in his 27th year.

Machine Gun Canucks

RONALD Gordon Campbell   Serv. # 2293451

Gordon was born on December 1st 1888 to James and Christa-Ann Ronald.

After finishing school Gordon worked on area farms and went out west on harvest excursions. They would thresh from August to Christmas. He also spent a couple of winters in logging camps in Saskatchewan and Vancouver Island.

Gord joined the Lord Strathcona Horse in 1914. He was a good musician and sometimes entertained his buddies with a few tunes on the flute. He served in France and Belgium for 18 months and with the machine guns, the mud, and the artillery the cavalry often had to fight on foot.

On November 9th 1917 16 men from the Lord Strathconas were chosen to be half of the honour guard for the Lord Mayor of London's parade and Gord was chosen to be one of them. After the war Gord went back to Vancouver Island because the pay was much better.

In 1923 he bought a 1920 Harley Davidson motorcycle which he rode from Port Alberni, British Columbia to Long Island, New York in 1924. After the trip he decided to stay home. He married Mary Telfer Shiel and bought the Shiel farm just south of Plattsville on the 10th Concession. Their daughter, Margaret Evelyn, was born on August 21st 1928.

Gordon kept the Harley till the end of his life. His grandson, John McCabe of Ayr, now has it as a prized possession. Gord is on the right of the top row in the photo of the Machine Gun Canucks.

Gordon died on October 15th 1985.

RONALD William Daniel

Ronald was born to James and Christa-Ann Ronald in 1886. After graduating from school he worked on the home farm and went on harvest excursions to the west. He joined the army early on in the war and served in France with the Seventh Battalion of the Canadian Expeditionary Force (C.E.F.). He was promoted to Corporal. Ronald was very badly wounded and after a spell in hospitals at home he became a Stationery Engineer. He plied his trade in lumber mills in British Columbia and Northern Ontario. He was hired by a firm in Winnipeg when his war wounds caught up with him.

William died in the Military Ward of the Winnipeg General Hospital on July 5th 1929. He was 43 years of age.

ROPER William   Serv.# 141526

William's name is inscribed on the Cenotaph in Dickson's Corners and at Chesterfield. He was Missing In Action on the 15th of August 1917 while serving with the 21st Battalion of the Canadian Expeditionary Force (C.E.F.).

William has no known grave but his name is inscribed on the Vimy Ridge Memorial.

Chesterfield Cenotaph

Vimy Ridge

ROUTLY James Earl

Jim was born on November 15th 1924 in Bright to Guy Everett and Gladys Routly. After finishing school he went to work for the Canadian National Railway. In late 1943 he joined the Army and was posted to the Artillery.

In 1944 Jim was sent overseas and was in England when his brother Bill was shipped back to hospital in England from Italy. Jim then served in France with the Artillery. After Victory in Europe (V.E.) Day he was sent into Germany as a member of our occupation forces.

In late 1946 Jim was sent home and given his honourable discharge.

Jim returned to the Canadian National Railway (C.N.R.) as an operator. In December 1950 he married Audrey E. Matheson and they had a son Robert on April 11th 1951. Jim was offered a position at Elliot Motors in Woodstock as Service Manager and decided to change employment.

Jim died in his 49th year on January 3rd 1973.

ROUTLY William Samuel

Bill was born on November 4th 1922 to Guy Everett and Gladys Routly.

On March 4th 1941 he joined the Royal Canadian Air Force (R.C.A.F.). He went to Manning Depot in Toronto and then Guelph for wireless training. He was then posted to Belleville for Bombing and Gunnery school. Bill suffered from air sickness so couldn't serve in air crew. He elected to take his discharge on April 15th 1942 and immediately joined the Oxford Rifles with Jacky Harmer on April 21st 1942. "A" Company was formed in Kitchener and then sent to Prince George, British Columbia for training. Graham Fenn and Bill went down to Montana to try and get into paratroops, but it didn't work out. A draft from the Oxford Rifles under the command of Captain Ed Fergusson were posted to Debert, Nova Scotia and went overseas in February 1943. Bill was then attached to the Highland Light Infantry. He was hospitalized for Yellow Jaundice.

When he was released from hospital he was posted to the Princess Patricia Canadian Light Infantry. They were sent to Sicily and Italy for the invasion. Bill suffered a bad wound to his kneecap and after he recovered was sent back to his unit that were now attacking the Hitler Line. Fighting was fierce and only 18 out of the 800 in his unit survived injury or death. Bill lost the sight in his right eye and was also severely wounded in the right lung and right leg. He was in hospital in Italy for two months and then shipped to a hospital in England for a month or so.

After this he was sent to Canada on a hospital ship and on to Westminster Hospital in London, Ontario where he spent the next year. When he recovered he was discharged from the army on September 4th 1945.

Bill went back to Bright and opened a pool hall with snacks, cigarettes and ice cream. On August 17th 1946 he was married to Lucille Ann MacKay. Together they converted the pool hall into a grocery store. Their only child, a son Ronald, was born on May 31st 1952

In 1948 Bill was hired by the Federal Department of Agriculture to inspect fruit and vegetables bound for export or canning factories. He and his family continued to live in Bright.

Bill had a heart attack in 1983 so at 61 years of age had to retire. He and Lucille moved to a very comfortable apartment in Woodstock where they still reside in 2003.

ROE James R.

Jim was born in England on June 25th 1872. He emigrated to Canada and went into agricultural labour as a hired man. He joined the Canadian Expeditionary Force in the First World War.

When he was discharged after the war he went back into farm labour. Stan Rennick and Jim were the best of friends. Jim worked for Frank King as a hired man for many years.

Jim died in Westminster Hospital in London, Ontario on February 28th 1949. The Royal Canadian Legion ordered and paid for the funeral. They also bought a burial plot in the Chesterfield Cemetery and the headstone.

SANGWIN John Troyer Serv.# 2009305

Jack was born on November 13th 1897 to Mrs Ida Sangwin in Plattsville, Ontario.

He was a store keeper in Plattsville and joined the Canadian Army on May 10th 1918. He was 5 feet 5 1/2 inches tall. The girth of his chest when fully expanded was 36 inches. The range of expansion was 5 inches. He had a fresh complexion with grey eyes and fair hair. Jack was a Methodist.

This picture was taken on August 11th 1919 in Plattsville.

After the war Jack moved out west and went into the lumber business. On July 3rd 1926 he married Martha Lillian English.

Jack died on June 24th 1964.

SAUNDERS Lewis Frederick   Service # A603272

Lewis was born on October 10th 1914 to Frederick and Hannah Saunders. He finished school in 1928 and went into agricultural work. He joined the Militia on November 24th 1942 and transferred to the permanent force in May 1944. Lewis went overseas and was wounded in France. After treatment he recovered and rejoined his unit on through France, Belgium and Holland. Lewis came home and received his discharge on August 2nd 1946. He lived in Woodstock for two and a half years and did construction and farm work.

On November 30th 1946 Lewis married Florence Marguerite Pellow. In April 1949 they rented the Stewart Gillespie farm on Lot 20 on the 12th Concession just a little west of Plattsville. Lewis also started to work at Canada Sand, as the farm didn't require all his time. On January 29th 1948 a daughter, Joyce Marguerite, was born. She was followed by Sharon Ann on April 24th 1949. Diana Louise showed up on January 17th 1952. Florence then surprised herself and Lewis with twin girls, Shirley Jane and Sheila May, born on April 10th 1956. Lewis was thrilled when Florence presented him with a son, Robert Lewis Frederick, on January 11th 1958.

In 1963 Lewis bought the farm they were renting under the Veterans Land Act (V.L.A.). They paid the V.L.A. loan off in 1993. Their son now owns the farm.

In 1995 the Dutch Government struck a medal and awarded it to all Canadians who fought in Holland and liberated them. Because of his service in Holland, Lewis was awarded this medal. Florence is very proud of it.

Lewis died on November 24th 2000 at Woodingford Lodge in his 87th year. Florence has her own apartment in New Dundee and spends time with members of the family who live in the area. She is also active in the community.

SCOTT

We have no information on Mr. Scott other than this picture taken on August 11th 1919. We do not even know his given name.

SCOTT Russell Cavin Serv.# R209881

Russell was born on March 1st 1924 to John and Amy Scott on a farm north of Bright. After finishing school he worked for a few months at Canada Sand and on March 3rd 1943 joined the Royal Canadian Air Force (R.C.A.F.). Russell was posted to Manning Depot in Toronto. This was located in the Exhibition Grounds and many of the pig and cattle barns were utilized for sleeping quarters. Naturally they were cleaned up and modified for the airmen.

From Manning Depot he was posted to Initial Training School (I.T.S.) at Victoriaville in Quebec. On completion of his I.T.S. he was sent to Fingal for Bombing and Gunnery School and then to Crumlin Air Navigation School. His Bombing and Gunnery class was then posted to Three Rivers in Quebec for a Battle Course.

On the 21st of July 1944 he sailed from Halifax on the Nieu Amsterdam. Bournemouth had been emptied of airmen for the invasion, so they went to Infoworth in Gloustershire for a short stay, then to Bournemouth. He was posted to Northern Ireland for Advanced Flying Unit (A.F.U.) then to Honeybourne for Operational Training on Wellington Bombers. The next stop was Conversion unit at Topcliffe where the crew was completed and they converted to four motor bombers, in this case the Halifax Mark 111 which had radial motors that gave it more height and speed than the Mark 11 and Mark V which had in line Rolls Royce Merlin motors. They then joined 408 squadron at Linton-on-Ouse.

By this time the war was wound up so in June 1945 he came back to Canada to train for the Pacific, but the A Bomb then knocked the Japanese out of the war.

Russell received his discharge on November 19th 1945 and then went to Rehabilitation School in Hamilton where he took up construction. After his training he settled in Kitchener and was employed by Ed. Witmer and Sons as Superintendent of construction.

On August 2nd 1952 Russell married Grace Marion Bean. They had three children starting with Lorie Jane born March 11th 1959. Lois Ann arrived on June 2nd 1962 followed by Brian Robert on April 30th 1966.

Russell also worked for Incom Construction and is still, in 2003, involved in consulting work.

SCOTT Thomas John

Thomas was born on October 17th 1919 to John and Amy Scott on a farm north of Bright. After finishing school John took up agricultural work at the home farm and also on neighbourhood farms. In the summer of 1940 Tom joined the Royal Canadian Service Corps. After several months of training he was posted overseas in 1941 and participated in the invasion of Italy.

After fighting their way up the Italian Peninsula his unit was transferred to France and then Belgium and Holland. Tom came home in October 1945 and received his honourable discharge soon after.

He then started working at construction in Kitchener. After a couple of years he went to Toronto and got a job in the Express Division of the Canadian Pacific Railway (C.P.R.). He retired from the C.P.R. in the late 1980's.

Thomas died on May 5th 1994.

Russell   Thomas

SCOTT William

Plattsville Memorial Gates

Bill served one year and nine months as a corporal in the Regina Rifles Regiment. He was sent overseas in July 1944 and saw service in Belgium, Holland and Germany.

Bill was included in the write up which the Plattsville Girl Guides made in their Victory Post written in 1946.

SEEGMILLER Ezra Henry

Ezra was born on February 2nd 1913 to William and Eda of Chesterfield. After finishing school Ezra worked on the family farm and did custom work for area farmers.

In 1940 he joined the army and served in London and Petawawa.

After receiving his discharge in late 1945 Ezra worked in agriculture. Shortly after he was hired by Cities Service Oil Company of Woodstock. On June 18th 1955 Ezra married Norah Jones.

He was trimming the branches off a huge willow tree on his lot, when he tragically slipped and fell thirty feet to his death on April 16th 1966.

SEEGMILLER George Emil

George was born on December 1st 1917 to William and Eda on their farm near Chesterfield. After completing school George worked on the family farm and did custom work for other farmers.

He joined the army in early 1940 and served in London and was transferred to Petawawa shortly after. On August 13th 1942 George married Lyla Milark. George received his discharge in late 1945 and he and Lyla settled in the Golden Lake area near Petawawa.

George had his own trucking business and was also employed at the United Cooperatives of Ontario in Eganville and sometimes worked at Hiedeman's Sawmill.

A son, Lawrence George, was born to George and Lyla on May 13th 1949. George was very active in the Eganville Branch of the Royal Canadian Legion. He was well known for calling square dances and both he and Lyla were talented musically. The week before his death George was presented with an Award of Merit by the Royal Canadian Legion, the highest award they bestow.

George died on May 2nd 1993.

SHANTZ Cameron Gillis   Serv # V47375

Cam was born June 14th 1922 to Abiah and Della (nee-Cressman) Shantz on the family farm outside Plattsville. When he graduated from high school he took employment in an office in Kitchener but after a year decided he preferred farm work. He joined the navy on December 3rd 1942 in Hamilton. He was assigned to the Engine Room Artificer (E.R.A.) course and after completion in October was sent to Toronto to take instruction on Internal Combustion. After completion he was posted to Esquimalt, British Columbia for nine months to take an advanced E.R.A. course.

After all this training Cam was posted to the H.M.C.S. Kootenay, one of our best destroyers, which was docked in Shelbourne, Nova Scotia. The crew assisted in refitting the ship and in January 1945 they assumed convoy duties from Canada to Europe. In really rough weather many of the crew got seasick, so those who didn't enjoyed double rations of food and navy rum. In the English Channel Submarines would hide by charted wrecks to escape detection. Some leaves were served in Northern Ireland and Cam and his buddies would go to Lifford in the Irish Free State to enjoy bacon and eggs at Ma Kennedy's. She kept a log of all Canadian sailors who lost their lives in the Battle of the Atlantic.

The day after the war ended Churchill ordered all German submarines to surface where they were and surrender to the nearest ship. Cam's ship had been out all night chasing a sub that sank a little minesweeper. They had the pleasure of accepting its surrender, it was the first of the German subs to surrender. On their arrival at headquarters in Londonderry many surrendered German subs were lined up in long rows. The next two months Cam spent in Nova Scotia aboard the New Waterford. Cam received his discharge on October 5th 1945.

While in the navy Cam married Marjorie Mildred Brown on August 18th 1943. They had two daughters, Judith Ann born on July 18th,1945 and Jane Agnes born on January 29th 1947. After his discharge Cam went out to Saskatchewan and farmed with an uncle for two years. He then returned to Ontario and took employment with the Harmer Brothers in Plattsville doing their sheet metal work. The position of Postmaster became vacant in 1960. Cam wrote the competitive exams and was duly appointed Postmaster.

Cam was always heavily involved with the community. He was a member of the Board of Trade and served as school trustee when the new school was built in Plattsville. He also became involved in horse farming and took over the Plattsville Horse Show. It became one of the top horse shows in the province. Cam also showed and sold his horses in American and Australian shows.

Cam erected five historical plaques on the main street (Albert Street) in Plattsville. He and Marj moved to New Hamburg after Cam suffered a stroke in 1999. In 2003 Cam is still showing his horses.

SHANTZ David

Plattsville Memorial Gates

David was born to Mr. & Mrs. Roy Shantz around 1927 in Plattsville. David joined the army on July 20th 1945. He was stationed at London and Vernon, British Columbia. David volunteered for the Pacific war but as it ended he took his honourable discharge.

David moved to British Columbia and went into landscaping.

SHANTZ Gilbert

Plattsville Memorial Gates

Gilbert was born to Mr. and Mrs. Roy Shantz around 1922. He trained at Camp Borden in Ontario and Debert, Nova Scotia.

He was posted to England in February 1944. He went into France on D Day and fought in France, Belgium and Holland as a sniper. Gilbert was seriously wounded in Holland while in the Army Tank Corps.

Gilbert came home in late 1945 and received his honourable discharge. Shortly after he moved to Alaska.

SHANTZ Grace Hilda

Grace was born on January 29th 1924 to Areli Edgar and Effie (nee-Moyer) Shantz at the home farm on the 14th Concession. She took her schooling in Plattsville and then went into housework in Galt. A year of this was plenty so Grace took a machinist course in Kitchener. After successful completion of the course she went to work at the Sunshine Company factory in Waterloo making smoke bombs.

On November 20th 1942 Grace joined the Canadian Womens Army Corps in London. She was 5 feet 7 inches tall with light brown hair and blue eyes. She took her basic training in Kitchener and was then posted to Camp Ipperwash, where she worked in Q.M. stores. After 12 months Grace was posted to the Westminster Hospital in London, Ontario as a guard in the Women's Section.

On June 6th 1944 she met her future husband, Clement Arthur Couture, who was a patient in the hospital. They were married on December 8th 1944. Grace received her honourable discharge on June 17th 1945.

On January 8th 1946 Clifford Ivan was born followed by Brian Clement on September 18th 1947. Roland Douglas joined the family on August 24th 1948 and then Wayne David appeared on November 7th 1949. Barbara Lynn, the only daughter, was delivered on July 1st 1955. Grant Mark was born on July 1st 1957. He was killed in a tragic motorcycle accident in Vancouver on August 14th 1983. Kevin Bradley completed the family on May 30th 1960.

Clement worked at Seagrams for 38 years. He died on October 5th 1998.

In 2003 Grace still lives in Preston.

SHANTZ Irene Elizabeth

Irene was born on January 2nd 1917 to Areli Edgar and Effie (nee-Moyer) Shantz in the home farm just outside Plattsville. She took her public and high school in Plattsville and then went into nursing at the K-W Hospital in Kitchener graduating in 1939.

She practiced private nursing until she joined the forces as a nursing sister in early 1943. Irene, at six feet tall was a striking young lady. She was posted overseas shortly after and served in two military hospitals in England. She nursed some of the wounded boys from the Highland Light Infantry (H.L.I.) who had known Ivan, her brother. When the war ended she was posted back to Canada and was given her honourable discharge.

In late 1945 Irene married Edward Lescom and they moved to Noranda, Quebec for a few years where Irene continued her nursing career. Irene and Edward had one daughter they named Cheryl Jennifer born on July 30th 1953. They then returned to Kitchener where Irene rejoined the K-W Hospital.

Irene died on March 2nd 1993.

SHANTZ Ivan Ray

Ivan was born on November 30th 1921 to Areli Edgar and Effie (nee Moyer) Shantz in the home farm on the 14th Concession of Blenheim Township just outside Plattsville.

After finishing school he did agricultural work in the area. In early 1942 Ivan joined the army and took his basic training at Camp Borden. After further training he joined the Highland Light Infantry and went overseas with them. Ivan went in with his unit on the D-day attack.

On July 8th 1944 Ivan was killed at Buron near Caen and is buried in the Beny-Sur-Mer Cemetery. His name is also inscribed on the Plattsville Cenotaph.

Beny-Sur-Mer Cemetery

SHANTZ Jacob Elgin

Elgin was born to Areli and Effie Shantz on September 12th 1922 on the home farm on the 14th Concession just outside Plattsville. After completing his schooling in Plattsville he went into beekeeping setting up an apiary near Ayr.

In February of 1942 he sold his bees and joined the Royal Canadian Air Force (R.C.A.F.) After a stint in Manning Depot in Toronto he was posted to St. Thomas where he was trained as an aero engine mechanic. He was extremely capable and was posted overseas and wound up working on Lancaster Bombers in the Wolf Squadron.

When the War ended he was posted back to Canada to The Pas in Manitoba. Elgin received his honourable discharge at the end of 1945 and worked on a family farm near Elmira. He finally took a farm near Rothesay.

In the fall of 1946 Elgin married Evelyn Graham from the Owen Sound area. They had three children, Linda, Lorna and an adopted son, Kenneth.

Elgin died on June 2nd 1984.

SHANTZ William Donald Moyer

Donald was born on the home farm to Areli and Effie Shantz on August 6th 1919. When he finished his schooling in Plattsville he went into agricultural work on the home and local farms. Don joined the Royal Canadian Air Force (R.C.A.F.) in the spring of 1941. After Manning Depot in Toronto he trained as an aero engine mechanic at the station in St. Thomas.

On successful completion of his course he was posted to Calgary and worked on Anson and Harvard aircraft. He later was posted to Yorkton, Saskatchewan and then Summerside in Prince Edward Island.

Don received his honourable discharge late in 1945. He moved to Toronto and started a career as a taxi driver. On December 26th 1946 Don married Margaret Helen Tuft. He prospered in the taxi business and wound up owning two taxis. Don and Margo had three children. George Randy was born on February 26th 1955 followed by Keith Douglas who arrived on June 8th 1956. Tracey Evelyn completed the family on October 9th 1959.

Donald died in 1991.

SHEARER Agnes Jean

Agnes was born on September 27th 1924 in Brantford, Ontario to Robert and Jeannie (nee-Black) Shearer. She was academically gifted and skipped a grade in Elementary School. After finishing school she did domestic work and worked on threshing gangs.

She joined the Canadian Women's Army Corps (C.W.A.C.) in late 1942, after the harvest. She was posted to Wainwright, Alberta and spent the Christmas of 1942 there. After initial training she was posted to Ottawa and remained there for the rest of the war working at C.W.A.C. headquarters.

She received her honourable discharge in late 1945.

Agnes died of cancer on January 26th 1946.

SHEARER John George

John was born on July 14th 1898 to William and Agnes (nee-Baird) Shearer. After completing school John worked on the home farm. John joined the army in 1915 and was posted overseas. He was sent to France in time to get involved in the first gas attack at Ypres in April 1915.

After receiving his honourable discharge in 1919 he bought a farm one mile east of Bright which he farmed for the rest of his working life. He raised grain crops, milk cows, some beef, chickens and eggs.

On August 14th 1924 John married Alma Marguerite Mulga from Bright. Their first son, George Ross was born on February 21st 1925. He was followed by William James born on June 9th 1926. William died of pneumonia on March 14th 1927. Douglas Mulga arrived on October 21st 1928. On April 11th 1932 the first girl, Margaret Agnes was born. Fredrick Hugh then arrived on November 9th 1933. The family was completed on August 8th 1937 with the birth of another daughter, Mary Isabella.

John and Alma retired in 1960 and moved into the Milgau house in Bright, while Fred took over the farm. Alma died on September 5th 1970 leaving John to fend for himself. In 1978 he moved into the Bonnie Brae Nursing Home in Tavistock.

John died on December 22nd 1983.

SHEARER Robert Millar

Robert was born on January 20th 1893 to William and Agnes (nee-Baird) Shearer. After finishing school he worked in agriculture at the home farm and other farms in the area. He also went out west on harvest excursions.

He joined the army in early 1915 and after some training was sent overseas. Bob met a beautiful young lady, Jean Black by name, in London, England. They were married on November 27th 1919. When he returned home he went out to Saltcoats, Saskatchewan and bought a farm under the Soldier Settlement Program.

Bob and Jean had a son, Robert Black born on August 27th 1920. Agnes Jean arrived on December 27th 1924. Tragically young Robert fell under the wheel of a wagon his father was driving and was killed. Margaret Jeanette completed the family on August 18th 1926.

Robert died on January 6th 1950. His wife Jean died in 1992 at 102 years of age.

SHEARER Russell Gordon

Russell was born on March 11th 1911 to William and Agnes (nee-Baird) Shearer. After completing his elementary schooling in Bright he went to Plattsville Continuation School and then to Ontario Agricultural College (O.A.C.) at Guelph for University. On graduation he was employed at the Blenheim News Tribune and soon became a partner in the enterprise. On June 15th 1939 Russ married Grace Warwick. Their first son, Donald Russell, was born on June 21st 1940.

In 1942 Russ joined the Royal Canadian Army Service Corps and received his commission as a Second Lieutenant. He was posted overseas in January of 1943 shortly after being promoted to First Lieutenant.

In 1943 his unit in the Service Corps was posted to Italy. During his service in Europe Russell was promoted to Captain. He came home in October of 1945 and on November 4th all eight brothers were at the home farm in Bright for the first reunion since 1915.

Russ received his honourable discharge in 1946 and went back to the Blenheim News Tribune. William Thomas completed the family on August 28th 1946. A few years later Russ bought his partner out and continued on until his retirement. He and Grace retired to Victoria, British Columbia and both sons relocated with them.

Russ died on November 7th 1978. At Russell's specific request the funeral was held at the Salvation Army Church with interment in the Victoria Cemetery.

SHEARER Thomas Edwin

Thomas was born on February 15th 1896 to William and Agnes (nee-Baird) Shearer. After completing school Tom worked in agriculture on the home farm and other farms in the area. He also went out west on harvest excursions. He joined the army in 1917 and served overseas.

Tom received his honourable discharge in 1919. Shortly after he bought the first farm north of Bright under the Soldiers Settlement Program. All farms were mixed in those days so they raised grain, had both beef and dairy cows and raised chickens for both the eggs and the meat.

Tom married Abigail Hunt on September 7th 1921. Their first child, Jean Elizabeth, was born on March 17th 1926. James William completed the family on May 16th 1932.

Thomas continued farming until his death on February 27th 1958. At this time Abigail was teaching at Greens School north of Chesterfield. From 1963 to 1968 she taught school at the Community Farm of the Brethren, one mile south of Washington. She was very highly thought of by the Brethren.

Abigail died on October 28th 1992.

SCHOSENBERG Donald Craig

Donald was born on November 13th 1920 to Harry and Sarah Eleanor Schosenberg in Bright. After completing his high school education in Plattsville he worked with his father at the turnip farm and plant. Donald married Laura Fay Astride from Wilberforce in the fall of 1940. A daughter, Donna Fay, was born to Laura and Donald on July 27th 1941.

Donald enlisted in the army at Woodstock on April 8th 1942. In due course he was posted overseas and was wounded in France. After the war ended he was shipped home and received his honourable discharge on November 1st 1946.

He was awarded The Canadian Volunteer Service Medal and Clasp, The Defence Medal, The 1939 1945 Star and The France Germany Star. He and Laura settled in Bright where he rejoined his father in the turnip business. Donald also started a small trucking company.

He sold the company after five years and drove for Active Cartage for three years. He then was hired as an immigration officer at Peace Bridge and moved to Fort Erie. Donald retired in 1980 and he and Laura moved to their cottage in Harcourt near Wilberforce. He became very active in the Legion and served as President of the Wilberforce Branch for many years.

Donald died on April 22nd 1995.

SIMONDS Robert Junior   Serv. # J29080

Bob was born on March 31st 1918 in Toronto, Ontario. After finishing high school he worked at the Ontario News where he met his future wife, Alice Isabel Elder. They were married on August 7th 1943. In due course they had four daughters. Joanne Margaret was born on May 29th 1944. Donna Jean followed on February 11th 1946, then Merilyn Alice appeared on September 25th 1949. The family was completed with the birth of Virginia May on July 11th 1955.

Bob joined the Royal Canadian Air Force (R.C.A.F.) on March 19th 1941. He served in Galt till July 14th when he was transferred to Manning Depot in Toronto for a scant month. He was posted from Toronto to Winnipeg until November when he was sent to Initial Training School in Regina, Saskatachewan from November 8th 1941 to February 6th 1942.

He was then posted to #15 Elementary Flying Training School in the same area. In due course he graduated from that and was posted to Service Flying Training School in Brandon till August 6th, 1943 when he received his pilots wings and his commission as a Pilot Officer. He was then posted to Air Navigation School in Rivers, Manitoba. Bob was appointed an instructor and trained other airmen at stations in Souris, Virden and Gimli, Manitoba and Davidson and Yorkton in Saskatchewan.

Bob received his honourable discharge in October 1945. He and his wife settled in Winnipeg and he worked for Van Kirk Decorating and Design. In the winter of 1949 Bob and his family moved to Plattsville where he worked for a few months as a freelance window dresser, a Coca-Cola truck driver and a vacuum cleaner salesman.

In 1950 Bob was hired by Canada Sand Papers as a lab technician and was promoted to Quality Control. Bob was extremely capable and after Carborundum Abrasives bought the plant they sent Bob to Campinas, Brazil to supervise a new Carborundum plant where he was instrumental in producing a quality product under adverse conditions. His family followed and they spent five years in Brazil.

In 1961 they returned to Plattsville. Bob was promoted to management positions and in 1983 he retired as General Manager. He then indulged his hobbies of sailing, exploring cyberspace on his computer and building toys and furniture for his children and grandchildren. He also kept adding to his sophisticated model train layout.

His wife Alice died on September 8th 1995. Bob was diagnosed with cancer of the pancreas and lungs early in 2000. He passed away at the age of 83 on November 26th 2001.

SIMPSON John Stanley Service # A 82022

John was born on August 15th 1904 in North Dumfries Twp. He grew up in Perry's Corners where he attended school. John went to work at Dave Hall's in 1920. He worked at various agricultural jobs before finally settling on a factory job at Canada Sand.

John married Merle Stuart on April 8th 1933. Merle was born on August 14th 1904, so she was one day older than her husband. They moved to Washington immediately after marriage and in due course had three children. A daughter, Dorothy Madeline was born on July 7th 1933. Two sons followed, William Stuart on April 29th 1935 and Robert Keith born January 3rd 1937.

John enlisted in the Oxford Rifles on April 6th 1942 at Woodstock, Ontario. He was stationed in London and Prince George, British Columbia for training and in the beginning of 1943 went overseas with the British Columbia Dragoons. He then served in the United Kingdom, Sicily, Italy, France, Belgium and Holland.

He returned home in December of 1945 and received his honourable discharge on January 19th 1946. John was awarded the 1939-45 Star, Italy Star, France and Germany Star, and the Canadian Volunteer Service Medal with Clasp. Shortly after discharge he started back to Canada Sand.

Merle predeceased John, she died on October 3rd 1974. John Stanley died on October 26th 1977 in his 74th year.

SINCLAIR Frederick Albert   Serv.# SA 1185

Fred was born on November 9th 1930 at the Sinclair farm on Lot 17 on the 11th Concession, Blenheim Township. He joined the army in London in early January of 1951 and was sent to Currie Barracks in Calgary, Alberta. Fred was put in the holding company and received his basic training at the Calgary stampede grounds. Advanced training was given at Currie Barracks. In July he was posted to Wainwright Alberta on policing duty. Assignment to the 1st Battalion Princess Patricia Canadian Light Infantry followed in August. Fred was sent home on leave and was returned on assignment to Korea. The unit was shipped out from Seattle, Washington in August of 1951.

The people of South Korea supported our troops. Of course the North and South Koreans were identical and as the United Nations force was occidental, orientals in the front line were carefully screened. Both Chinese and North Korean troops were poorly trained. Their one advantage was large numbers. Leaves (Rest and Recreation) were usually of seven days duration and always taken in Tokyo. Fred had two leaves while in Korea and spent them in Tokyo. The Japanese were very friendly and did what they could to entertain our men. Bob Hope and Doris Day used to make trips to the East to entertain the troops. They were very popular.

In October 1952 Fred left Korea and returned to Vancouver after 399 days served in Korea. He returned home on 60 days leave and then back to Calgary to rejoin his unit.

In January of 1953 he was sent to Rivers, Manitoba for parachute training. Fred reminisced, we were lined up for parade and the Sergeant in command was doing roll call and assigning us to barracks. When he came to my name he said, "Sinclair when I break the men off, you stay." Naturally I was trying to think of what I had done wrong. He then told me while shaking hands that he knew me from gathering milk from the farms where I grew up. This man was Sergeant Hewitt Quick from Bright. He had served in the First Canadian Parachute Battalion in the Second World War. At this point I knew I had it made with Sergeant Quick as my instructor. After the full training, including six qualifying jumps, Fred received his paratroop wing and was then sent to Camp Borden on a sniper and scout course. When Fred returned to Calgary in June 1954 he was given his discharge.

On June 26th 1954 Fred married Mildred Hazel Pettigrew and returned to the Village of Bright. They have three children, Brian Ross was born on July 27th 1955, Sheila Diane followed on April 16th 1958 and Carolyn Jean completed the family on September 26th 1961.

Fred took up the trade of an electrician. In 2003, Fred still resides in Bright.

SMITH Kenneth Walter

Kenneth was born on September 30th 1912 to Walter and Melvina Smith of Plattsville. After finishing school in the late twenties he went to work at the J. B. English General Store in Plattsville and a few years later went to Canada Sand. On May 17th 1941 he married Margaret Rose Baird.

In July 1941 he joined the Canadian Fusiliers, City of London Regiment. After initial training in London and Camp Borden he was transferred to the Sudbury and Sault Ste. Marie Regiment. They were then stationed in Vernon, British Columbia and Ozada where they guarded German prisoners of war.

He returned to the Fusiliers who took up duty at Kiska in the Aleutian Islands in August 1942. The Japanese had reconnoitred the Aleutians and we expected an invasion. Around this time the Japanese released balloons with bombs attached. They released them off the Canadian coast and hoped for some damage and deaths, fortunately none occurred. Ken later returned to Nanaimo, Prince George, Vernon and other camps in British Columbia. He received training in carpentry during his British Columbia service. Ken was stationed at Prince Rupert at the time he received word his daughter Kenna Margaret was born.

He went on furlough from October 2nd to the 27th in 1944 and then back to British Columbia. He received his discharge in early 1946.

After his discharge he went back to Canada Sand for a short while, and then went with Alex Glendinning building houses in Brantford. He went back to Canada Sand in 1950 and stayed until his retirement in August of 1977. Margaret Rose died on December 13th 1974.

Ken married Anna Elizabeth Waldie on March 28th 1980.

Kenneth died on November 24th 1998.

Kiska

STAUFFER Gordon Henry   Serv. # 781099

Gordon was born on June 11th 1889 to Mr. & Mrs. Daniel R. Stauffer on his father's farm east of Chesterfield. He was employed as a Bank Clerk in Kitchener and served in the 108th Regiment of the militia. On the 10th of November 1915 Gordon joined the 118th Battalion of the Canadian Expeditionary Force (C.E.F.) and after infantry training was posted overseas. He was 5 feet 8 1/2 inches tall. His chest girth fully expanded was 35 inches with a range of expansion of 3 inches Gordon was of medium complexion with brown eyes and dark hair.

He was killed in action on November 6th 1917 while serving in the 1st Battalion of the C.E.F. Gordon has no known grave. His name is inscribed on the Menin Gate Memorial MR29. His name is also inscribed on the Cenotaphs at Dickson's Corners and Chesterfield.

Menin Gate Memorial

STEEDSMAN George Frederick Serv. # 675096

Bruay Communal Cemetery

Chesterfield Cenotaph

George was born near Ratho on June 17th 1897. His father was David Steedsman who later moved to R.R. #1 St. Marys, Ontario.

George enlisted on January 8th 1916, giving his trade as 'Shellmaking'. He was 5 feet 9 inches tall with a chest girth of 35 inches fully expanded with a range of expansion of 3 inches. He had a medium complexion, blue eyes and light brown hair. He also had a large scar under the little finger of his left hand. He was a member of the Presbyterian church.

George died of wounds on August 18th 1917 while serving with the 21st Battalion of the Canadian Expeditionary Force. He is buried in the Bruay Communal Cemetery Fr. #32. He is named on the Cenotaph in Victoria Park in Woodstock and the Cenotaph in the Chesterfield churchyard.

STEMMLER Frank

Plattsville Memorial Gates

Frank served three years in the Medical Corps of the Navy. He married a Scottish girl. He served on the H.M.C.S. Brockville and later was stationed in the Navy Hospital in Halifax doing office work.

Frank was included in the Victory Post 1946 listing by the Plattsville Girl Guides.

STEWART John James

Jim was born on April 16th 1918 to John Henry and Millicent Rachel Stewart. After finishing school he did agricultural work on the home farm and in 1938 was hired to work at the Baird dairy farm who specialized in Jersey cows.

In 1940 he joined the Oxford Rifles and after due training was posted out west. At the end of the war he was sent home and received his honourable discharge. He bought the old Waldie farm on Lot 23 and part of Lot 22 on Concession 13 of Blenheim Township under the Veterans Land Act. It was 48 acres so in 1952 Jim went to work for Canada Sand and treated the farm as more or less a hobby farm.

On September 10th 1949 Jim married Janet Small Smith. On December 24th 1952 they were blessed with twin daughters, Janet Elizabeth and Joan Alexandria.

Jim became active in the community and was elected as a school trustee. He was still serving on the School Board when the new school was built in Plattsville in 1961 consolidating Plattsville, Blink Bonnie and Washington. Additions were made to the building in 1965 and the Upper and Lower Tenths, Perry's Corners and Hallman's schools also were accommodated. In 1983 Jim retired from Canada Sand.

Jim died on November 17th 1984.

STEWART Martin Alexander

Martin was born on May 17th 1916 to John Henry and Millicent Rachel Stewart. After finishing school he did agricultural work at home and on neighbouring farms.

After the war started Martin enlisted in the Royal Canadian Air Force (R.C.A.F.) and was trained as an aero engine mechanic. He worked on aircraft at various stations in Western Canada. He received his honourable discharge in the fall of 1945. He went back to the home farm and in due course bought it under the Veterans Land Act. He operated it as a dairy farm and had a herd of Holsteins.

Stewart enjoyed music and was a very good guitar player. In the war he often entertained his buddies in the Air Force with a little music. After the war he joined Harry Lee Davidson's band in Plattsville.

Martin died around 1996.

MEDALS AWARDED TO FRANCIS CATTO STOTT

1939 - 1945 STAR   **Ribbon - Navy Red & Blue**

The Atlantic Star   **Blue Silver & Green - France & Germany Clasp**

The North Africa Star   **Gold & Red - North Africa Clasp**

Defence Medal   **Orange & Green**

Canada Volunteer Service Medal and Clasp   **Navy & Red - Maple Leaf Clasp**

King George V1 1939 - 1945   **Red White & Blue**

The Russian Murmansk Medallion

STOTT Francis Catto

Frank was born on June 15th 1921 to James and Margaret Stott. After finishing school Frank turned his hand to any work available. He graded roads in the winter, hoed turnips and did farm work summer and fall.

He joined the Royal Canadian Navy in October 1941. He was posted to the naval station in London, H.M.C.S. Prevost, for elementary training and then sent to the east coast for shipboard duty. Frank served on the H.M.S. Leith, a Corvette. The complement on a Corvette was about 150 men. They were really a small destroyer, faster but not as heavily armed. They were primarily for convoy duty and charged with finding and sinking enemy submarines. Later he served on the H.M.S. Monnow, also a Corvette. This ship made two successful trips to Murmansk in Russia. Frank was on them both. The Murmansk run was brutal. It went away north past Norway to Northern Russia. Fleets of German subs were stationed in the Norwegian fjords and attacked the convoys constantly. Ninety percent of the merchant ships on Murmansk convoys were sunk, but the Russians were desperate for military supplies. If you were torpedoed no effort could be made to save you as any ship that stopped would be sunk for sure. The water was so cold a man died within two minutes of exposure. At this time Frank was a Petty Officer. On November 23rd 1988 Frank was presented with the Murmansk Medallion by the Russian Government.

At the war's end Frank was sent on leave, and on July 25th 1945 married Margaret Euphemia McDonald. With the declaration of Victory in Japan (V-J) Day on August 14th 1945 the services of our military were no longer needed so Frank was discharged in the fall of 1945. After his discharge he and Marg lived in a small house on his father's farm. Frank worked at whatever jobs he could get.

On June 1st 1947 Frank started working for Canada Sand in Plattsville. In 1952 Frank and Marg moved to Washington and rented half the big stone house across from Richmonds. Frank said it was as cold as charity in the winter.

In 1954 they bought the brick house just north of the United Church in Washington, and lived there till 1999. Frank and Marg had three children. John Allen was born on July 28th, 1947, Elizabeth Jean on February 3rd 1950 and Diana Leslie on May 9th 1955. Diana was tragically killed in a car accident on May 4th 1968.

Frank was very active in the community and his church. He was Chairman of the School Board when Plattsville, Blink Bonnie and Washington were consolidated in a new school in Plattsville. In 1965 additions were made to the school and four more schools were amalgamated, Perry's Corners, Hallman's, Upper Tenth and Lower Tenth.

Frank retired in 1986. He died on April 23rd 1993. In 2004, Margaret resides in a condominium at Winston Park in Kitchener.

STRACHAN Laidlaw Elgin

Laidlaw was born on February 26th 1923 to Howard and Adeline Strachan in Alberta. They moved to Bright where Laidlaw took his Public School education.

He then graduated from the Plattsville Continuation School in 1941 and after some work in agriculture he joined the Royal Canadian Air Force (R.C.A.F.) in the summer of 1942. He suffered from air sickness so had to transfer out of air crew. He went into munitions and instrument repair and maintenance. He was sent overseas in 1943 and posted to a Canadian Squadron. The Squadron was moved to France after the invasion. When the war ended Laidlaw was posted back to Canada and received his honourable discharge in the summer of 1945.

He came home and obtained employment at a steel plant in Preston. He met a young lady and became quite interested. On June 7th 1947 Laidlaw married Elizabeth Louise Constable. Laidlaw preferred the military life and in 1948 he rejoined the air force. He served in Trenton, Centralia, Calgary, Alberta, McDonald near Portage La Prairie in Manitoba and St. Hubert in Quebec. Linda Anne was born on December 14th 1949.

In March of 1953 he went to Zweibruecken with Squadron 416, a Canadian Fighter Squadron. He came back in the summer of 1954 to North Bay. Wayne Elgin completed the family on April 25th 1956. Laidlaw was then posted to St. Johns, Newfoundland. In 1964 he was moved to Summerside P.E.I. Laidlaw and the family loved Prince Edward Island. They stayed there until his honourable discharge in December of 1969.

Laidlaw died on September 9th 1981.

VANCE John Robert Serv. # A-109496

John was born on January 20th 1913 to Samuel and Elizabeth Ann Vance on the home farm west of Chesterfield. He attended the Ratho School, which was located on the Vance farm, and the Plattsville Continuation School. After finishing school he continued in agricultural work and got involved in tobacco farming. He worked at a tobacco farm near Gobles and later at a tobacco farm near Walsingham. John married Ruby Goff in 1940.

He joined up in January 1944 with the Lincoln and Welland Regiment. They trained at London, Woodstock, Brampton and Debert Nova Scotia. The Regiment was shipped to England in the last week of November 1944. He served in Belgium, Holland and Germany. John was killed on March 8th, his father's birthday, in 1945.

John is buried in the Canadian Military Cemetery near Nijmegen, Netherlands. His grave is located in Section 1V, Row G, Plot No. 4. His name is also inscribed on the Chesterfield Cenotaph.

VEITCH Frederick Walker   Serv. # 437888

Lijssentheok Military Cemetery

Fred was born to George Malcom and Annie Maria (nee-Walker) in 1892. He enlisted in Plattsville with the 51st Battalion.

He died of wounds on Thursday the 15th of June 1916 while serving with the 15th Battalion C.E.F. as a private. He was 24 years of age. Fred is buried in the Lijssentheok Military Cemetery Poperinghe, West-Vlaanderen, Belgium.

Fred's name is inscribed on the Cenotaph at Chesterfield.

Chesterfield Cenotaph

VEITCH Ross Walker

Ross was born to George Malcolm and Annie Maria (nee-Walker) Veitch on May 5th 1898. All the boys in the family were given the mother's maiden name as their middle name. He joined the 110th Battalion Canadian Expeditionary Force (C.E.F.) in London, Ontario on June 16th 1916 having just graduated from Normal School in Stratford on the honours list. He was 5 feet 8 inches tall, with black hair and blue eyes. Ross went overseas as a Corporal and was promoted to First Lieutenant while in France.

He came home in 1919 and received his honourable discharge. Shortly after receiving his discharge he was hired as a teacher at the Preston Public School. In July 1924 Ross was appointed Assistant Principal and in July of that year he married Velma Florence Kennedy. He was appointed Principal of the school in 1931. Ross and Velma had two daughters. Jessie Marie was born on October 19th 1925 and Roslyn Jeanne completed the family on April 28th 1939. In January 1941 Ross was appointed acting Postmaster of the Preston Post Office. In June of 1941 he was promoted to Postmaster.

Tragically Ross died of a brain tumour on April 28th 1943.

WALDIE Earl Scott

Earl was born on May 23rd 1919 to Bert and Jessie Waldie on the home farm near the Blink Bonnie School.

After finishing school Earl worked on his father's farm and some neighbouring farms. He also did trucking for Dan Stauffer. Earl joined the Royal Canadian Engineers in October of 1941. He was promoted to Lance Corporal and was in the army for 10 months. He was stationed at London, Kitchener and Petawawa during that time. He was honourably discharged for medical reasons in August 1942.

Earl came home and started to work for Canada Sand.

On June 24th 1944 he married Jane McIntyre. Their first child, Mary Jane, was born on October 26th 1947. Nancy Carol followed on August 10th 1951. Sharon Ann was born on January 28th 1953 and the only boy, Craig John followed on June 17th 1964. Earl retired from Canada Sand in 1983 when he and Jane moved to Kitchener.

Earl died on September 12th 1988.

WALLBANK William Arthur

Bill was born on September 14th 1925.

In 1941 Bill joined #143 Squadron Air Training Cadets and served till 1943. When Bill turned 18 in September of 1943 he joined the Royal Air Force (R.A.F.) and went into aircrew training as a wireless operator/air gunner. In July 1944 Bill received his Wireless Air Gunner (WAG) wing and was posted to #6 Advanced Flying Unit in Staverton Gloucester where he trained on Ansons, a twin engined bomber. In September Bill was posted to #12 Operational Training Unit (O.T.U.) at Banbury. They flew Wellington Bombers that were used on the First Thousand Bomber raid on Cologne Germany. In January Bill's crew converted to Lancaster Bombers at the Conversion Unit at Doncaster, completing their training in March of 1945.

They were then posted to #100 Squadron of No. 1 Bomber Group in Lincolnshire. Bill flew on the last bombing raid of the war. Two hundred bombers participated each with an 8,500 pound bomb load. Their target was Berchtesgarden, Hitler's lair in the Austrian Alps. They also made five food drops to Holland before the war ended.

In December 1945 Bill was sent to #40 Squadron on Lancasters at Abu Sueir, otherwise known as Ismalia, in Egypt until January 1946. His crew was then posted to #38 Squadron at Ein Shemer in Palestine, now Israel. Their main job was to intercept illegal immigrant vessels in the Mediterranean heading for Palestine. They located one vessel and had the Royal Navy intercept them and send them to Cyprus. The Jews were put in camps to await legal immigration. The number of immigrants was restricted, so they had to wait their turn.

Bill was demobilized in November 1947. On December 23rd 1949 Bill was married to Elizabeth Charlotte Cowley. On April 7th 1951 Graham John was born and on August 21st 1952 Susan Elaine Maher followed. The family was completed on September 21st 1959 with the arrival of Denise Anne.

In March of 1954 Bill emigrated to Canada and joined his brother in Plattsville. Bill had purchased some machinery in England for spring making and was instrumental in the start up of the Wallbank Spring Factory.

Bill joined Massey Ferguson in November 1974. He retired as Plant Superintendent in 1985.

Bill's medals are the 1939-1945 Star, France Germany Star, Defence Medal, the War Medal and the 1945-1948 Palestine Medal.

Bill and his wife now reside in Kitchener.

WALTER Arthur (Archie) William

Archie was born on December 4th 1924 to Emil and Annie Marie Walter in Bright. After completing his education in Bright Arthur obtained employment with Hay and Co. in Woodstock in 1938. In 1943 Arthur joined the Royal Canadian Air Force. He was trained in ground crew and posted overseas.

After the war he was sent back to Canada and received his honourable discharge in late 1945 and went back to Hay and Co. Shortly after they were taken over by Weldwood. In 1970 Archie left Weldwood and was appointed Manager of the Woodstock City Arena on Perry St. and shortly after was given responsibility for the Civic Centre Arena as well. The arenas were busy all year long with roller skating and lacrosse in the summer and skating, hockey and curling in the winter. He also belonged to the Naval Vets Association in Woodstock.

On December 18th 1946 Archie married Irma Julia Yecny. Their first child, Sharon Julia arrived on June 2nd 1949. She tragically died of meningitis on January 4th 1950. Linda Dianne came on March 12th 1952 followed by Brenda Lee on March 28th 1957. Carol Marie completed the family on May 14th 1958. Archie loved his daughters, who spoiled him rotten. He also loved fishing and had a trailer at Puslinch Lake.

Archie died of a heart attack on December 13th 1980.

Archie   Donald

WALTER Donald Emil Serv.# A-114088

Donald was born on July 3rd 1919 to Emil and Annie Marie (nee-Wharf) Walter in Bright. After finishing school Donald was employed by the Eureka Foundry and Manufacturing Co. in Woodstock. Donald married Helen Lottie Murray on May 11th 1940.

On June 1st 1943 he joined the 1st Battalion of Prince Albert volunteers and was posted to Port Alberni in British Columbia. After further training he was posted overseas and participated in the Italian campaign. On April 27th 1944 he lost his right lung from enemy fire. Donald received his honourable discharge on November 19th 1945. He went back to Eureka and stayed with them until he received his retirement in 1984.

Donald and Helen started their family with Donald George born on August 12th 1940. Betty Ann arrived on October 17th 1943 followed by Mary Ellen on May 23rd 1947. The family was completed by Karon Helen on April 15th 1956.

Donald loved horses and had a hobby of raising and showing Hackney horses. He started in 1958 with three that he stabled at the Woodstock fairgrounds. His daughter Mary shared his love and used to help him in caring for and showing his beauties. They showed them at fairs in Woodstock, Embro, Tavistock, New Hamburg, Leamington and some American shows.

He also loved fishing. Donald was active in the Woodstock Agricultural Society for many years and served as President for 1980-1981.

Donald died on March 29th 1994. Helen joined him on June 13th 1995.

WARWICK Arthur Ernest   Service #163951

Arthur was born on January 7th 1890 in Enfield, England. He came to Canada in the early 1900's as a home boy. He joined the 4th Battalion of the Canadian Expeditionary Force (C.E.F.) as a Private. Arthur married in 1917 to Mary (Mae) Winfield of Hastings, England. Mary was born in 1887 in Hasting, England. She had a son by a previous marriage, Ernie Ball. On September 26th 1918 Ivy May was born. A sister, Wilma, was born on September 22nd 1926.

This picture was taken on September 11th 1919 in Plattsville. Shortly after Arthur received his honourable discharge. His wife lived in Washington while Arthur was overseas and when he came home they moved into the house across from the blacksmith shop, which is now the garage. Arthur had a horse and a cow and worked on farms in the area. He worked a lot for Rufus Davidson on the 11th Concession and also for Bingeman. He also worked at Canada Sand for a short while. Mary died in December 1939. In 1941 Arthur married Dorothy Schafer from Kitchener. Arthur died of a heart attack on April 1st 1950 and is buried in the Chesterfield Cemetery.

WATT James

James was born in Scotland in 1884. He came out to Canada when quite young as a Home Boy. They were placed on farms to mature and work. Some farmers treated them as family and some treated them as indentured servants.

When the First World War came along he enlisted in the army and served in the 168th Battalion. After the war he came back to the Plattsville area and worked in agriculture as a hired man for the rest of his life.

Jim died in 1943 and his funeral was ordered and paid for by the Royal Canadian Legion. They also bought the headstone and burial plot in the Chesterfield Cemetery.

WILKINS Charles Hume

Hume was born in Hespeler on April 19th 1912. His mother died just hours after he was born. Through his early boyhood Hume was raised by his grandmother Wilkins. When Hume was nine his father married Olive Buchner and before long Hume had a sister Ruth and a brother Edgar, who died in 1983. When he was seventeen Hume contacted spinal meningitis, which in those days was almost always fatal. He received serum from the Toronto General Hospital and recovered.

After graduating from Galt Collegiate he spent a year at Central Baptist Seminary in Toronto and another year at Toronto Normal School. He then embarked on a teaching career. During the depths of the depression he worked a winter for Frontier College in lumber camps near Longlac, Ontario.

On June 1st 1940 Hume joined the Royal Montreal Regiment. Shortly after he married Norma Scholey of Toronto on July 6th 1940. Hume was trained at Valcartier and was an instructor on the old Water Cooled Vickers .303 machine gun. Hume was sent to Three Rivers with the Toronto Scottish and then posted for officer training to Brockville Ontario. He went overseas in April 1943 and wound up in the Inkerman Barracks at Woking. After training in England for six months his unit was sent to Algiers in November 1943 for tank training.

In April 1944 Hume and his unit were posted to Naples as reinforcements for the 1st Troop of Royal Canadian Dragoons. They were a reconnaissance unit and drove Stag Hounds, a very fast and heavily armed scout car used to reconnoitre enemy positions. At this time Hume received his Mentioned-in-Despatches, a not insignificant honour.

In the spring of 1945 the unit was transferred to N.W. Europe and served in Belgium, Holland and Germany. Hume was awarded The C.V.S.M. and Clasp, Italy Star, Mentioned-in Dispatches, France Germany Star, the 1939-1945 Star and the War Medal. Hume came home on the Pasteur and docked in Quebec City on the 12th of August 1945. Hume and Norma Scholey were married in July of 1940.

In late 1942 Hume and Norma adopted Susan Evangeline. Annabel Ruth and Charles Everett were born in the late 1940s. In 1948 Hume graduated with an Honours B.A. in English Literature from the University of Toronto. For the next 28 years he was involved with all aspects of education, even pioneering in educational television. In the early 1970s Hume earned his M.A. in Victorian Literature from the University of Toronto. Retiring in 1976 he and Norma moved to Plattsville. As always Hume became deeply involved with the church and the community.

He was active in the Young at Heart Club and the Heritage Committee. For years he wrote numerous stories for the Saturday Night, The Globe and Mail and The Family Herald. He wrote his first book of poetry in the late 1950s.

In Plattsville he wrote a widely read column for the Ayr News. On September 28th 1988 Norma died. Hume kept up his many community activities and in 1996 wrote a book "Winding River", which contained impressions of the early Plattsville Community to record two hundred years of early Plattsville History. In 1999, Hume received the first ever Community Participant Award from the Plattsville School Parents Association. This annual award was renamed the Hume Wilkins Community Participant Award in his honour.

Hume died on July 21st 2001. His life touched us all.

WILSON John Bingham

John was in The First Motor Machine Gun Brigade and was killed in action on October 30th, 1917. John has no known grave. His name is inscribed on the Menin Gate Memorial, the cenotaph in Chesterfield and Dickson's Corners.

Menin Gate Memorial

Chesterfield Cenotaph

WOOLCOTT Earl James   Serv.# A 3817

Earl was born on Lot 21, Concession 12, Blenheim Township to William and Janet Woolcott. He attended Blink Bonnie and the Upper Tenth schools. He went into agricultural work after finishing school and became the farm manager of the Prospect Farm on the Blandford-Wilmot Townline. Earl joined the army in March of 1940. Basic training was in London. He was posted overseas in July of 1940 in the infantry. While in England he was General McNaughton's driver. He was sent to Italy at the end of 1943 as a signalman and transport driver carrying troops and supplies through the Italian mountains. In February 1945 he sailed from Leghorn to Marseilles in France, then on to Belgium and finally the liberation of Holland. He arrived home on August 1945 and shortly after received his honourable discharge at London, Ontario.

Earl rented a farm at Embro for a year then in the fall of 1946 he and his brother Glen purchased adjoining farms on the 1st Concession of West Zorra under the Veterans Land Act. On June 7th 1947 Earl married Eileen Wilson Bell, a nurse working at the Woodstock General Hospital. Eileen came from Lamont, Alberta. They had three children. James Little was born on June 14th 1950, Barbara Bell arrived on December 30th 1954 and Margaret Irene completed the family on October 25th 1957.

Earl always had a keen interest in Clydesdale horses and had a string of his own for farm work. As a hobby he showed these at fall fairs and also lent them out for plowing matches. In 1952 he was asked to join the staff advertising for Wilson and Co., Meat Packers of Chicago. He toured the mid-western U.S. showing these colourful horses at international fairs, sporting events, opening of new stores and parades.

In 1955 he returned home and expanded his farming operation, but always retained a strong interest in the horse business. Pressure and economic change made him decide to give up farming in 1967 and he went to work for Anheiser Busch Corp of St. Louis with their many fine horses. During his last ten years with the company he was in charge of the east coast hitch with home base in Merrimack, New Hampshire.

After one heart attack and a mild stroke he returned to Canada to live with his family in Tavistock and later at R.R. #1 Bright. He was badly handicapped the last two years of his life. Earl died in Stratford General Hospital on February 4th 1984.

Earl was awarded the Canadian Volunteer Service Medal and Clasp the Defence Medal, The Italy Star, The France Germany Star and The 1939 - 1945 Star.

WOOLCOTT Glenn Bell   Serv. # A34897

Glenn was born on April 11th 1918 to William and Janet Woolcott.

In 1936 he started to work at the Baird dairy farm. They had a beautiful herd of Jersey cattle.

He joined the army in London on January 6th 1941 with the Oxford Rifles. He was sent to Sussex in New Brunswick where he trained for the artillery. In April of 1941 he was shipped overseas. Shortly after arriving in England he joined his brother Earl in the Royal Canadian Corps of Signals.

In November of 1943 they were sent to Sicily, but all of their equipment was sunk in the harbour they were using in Sicily. As a result they had to wait a month for replacement equipment. They landed in Italy in the Monte Cassino area. They then were with the troops all the way up to the Hitler line and provided equipment for communications with the troops even in no-man's-land. The fighting was brutal as it is very difficult to attack troops when they are dug in to mountainous terrain, as a result the whole Italian campaign was a nightmare.

In late 1944 they were moved from Naples to France. They supported the troops then through France and Belgium to Njimegen in Holland.

He arrived back in Canada on October 21st 1945 on the Isle de France. Glen was discharged from the service in November 1945. He bought a farm under the Veterans Land Act eight miles north of Ingersoll. He farmed there till 1953. Glen has always had a love of horses and was particularly drawn to the Clydesdale, the showiest draught horse in the world. He sold the farm and moved down to the states to look after and drive show teams. He met his wife down there, as she also had a great love for horses.

On November 19th 1966 Glen married Grace Adele Knuth.

He was with a couple of outfits and in 1968 was hired to look after, and drive, the Budweiser team and wagon. He was with them for 15 years driving in all the big shows, like the Rose Bowl parade and the Mardi Gras.

Glen finally retired in 1983 and came back to Ontario to live.

WRIGHT Benjamin   Serv. # 127378

Chesterfield Cenotaph

Benjamin enlisted on the 29th of September 1915 at Drumbo with the 71st Battalion. He died on Tuesday the 28th of December 1915 while serving with the 36th Battalion of the Canadian Expeditionary Force as a private. Benjamin is buried in the Shornecliffe Military Cemetery in Kent, England grave # 180.

His name is inscribed on the Cenotaph in Chesterfield.

His next of kin was George Wright of Priory Rd., Wrentham, Suffolk, England.

YECK William Bond

Bill was born on January 10th 1926 to Wilfred and Lois Yeck. Bill joined the Royal Canadian Navy Volunteer Reserve in November of 1943.

On December 23rd 1943 Bill married Elizabeth Ann Frier. She taught school on the lower 10th Concession. In March of 1944 Bill shipped out on Fairmile #113. This boat was a forerunner to the Motor Torpedo Boat. It was 90 feet long and 18 feet wide and could do 40 knots an hour. For armament they had 20 mm guns and of course depth charges. The Fairmile was made of plywood, two layers of 1 1/2 inches and a Rolls Royce motor. We had about ten of them. They didn't last too long, so they were replaced with Corvettes. After six months on the Fairmile, Bill was posted to one of two Canadian aircraft carriers. The Americans took a merchant ship and placed a flat steel deck on it. We had two of them. Bill served on one, the HMCS Puncher, till the end of the war. The other one was sunk. These were very primitive aircraft carriers and carried only 12 planes which were one engined Lysanders, a very slow reconnaissance aircraft. The carrier had large elastic bands stretched across the deck to be caught by hooks attached to the undercarriage and fuselage of the plane when landing. These helped to decelerate the plane so it would stop before going over the side.

One convoy trip Bill wound up in New York for a couple of days. He went to Saks Fifth Avenue and bought a beautiful dress for his wife. From New York they went across to Scotland and returned to Canada. Bill had a leave and took the dress to his wife. This is the picture of his wife wearing it. It certainly was a beautiful dress.

Bill made seven trips with convoys to England and Scotland. On one of the trips they went to Belfast. He received his honourable discharge in the fall of 1945.

Bill started his own construction business in Bright, and his wife taught school. On April 20th 1947 their first son, James William was born. Roderick John finally showed up on June 15th 1959 to complete the family. Bill had a thriving business and retired from construction in 1985.

Betty died on May 18th 2002 and shortly after Bill bought a house in Woodstock and in 2003 is living there and making improvements to the house. He is involved in community activties in Woodstock as well.

The picture beneath Bill and Betty was the mascot of the aircraft carrier Bill served on.

ZINIUK William Basilious Serv.# 119556

Bill was born on May 25th 1914 in Winnipeg, Manitoba.

Shortly after his family moved to Biggar, Saskatchewan where Bill met Laura Elizabeth Doan. Romance flourished and on September 30th 1939 William and Laura were married. They moved to South Porcupine in Ontario where Bill was hired to work in one of the Gold Mines in Timmins. Their first child, Gayle Patricia was born on January 20th 1941. Their second and last child, William Russell was born on March 9th 1943.

On November 24th 1943 Bill enlisted in the Royal Canadian Army Service Corps.

Laura moved back to Plattsville with the children. Bill was promoted to Corporal and sent overseas in early 1944. He served in England and Continental Europe. He was posted back to Canada in late 1945 and received his honourable discharge on March 12th 1946. Bill was awarded the 1939-1945 Star, the France Germany Star and the Canadian Volunteer Service Medal with Clasp.

He returned to Plattsville and after accepting a job with Central Housing and Mortgage Bill was moved to Sarnia. He was promoted to Building Inspector and retired in 1979 after 33 years service.

William died on February 5th 2001.

Please use these pages to record any family members or old friends you may wish to remember.

_____

_____

_____

_____

_____

_____

_____

_____

_____

_____

_____

_____

_____

_____

Please use these pages to record any family members or old friends you may wish to remember.

_____

_____

_____

_____

_____

_____

_____

_____

_____

_____

_____

_____